Family Child

D1531930

Contracts
& Policies

How to Be Businesslike
in a Caring Profession

Second Edition

Tom Copeland, J.D.

Redleaf Press
St. Paul, Minnesota

Disclaimer

This book discusses a variety of legal issues, including the role of contracts and other agreements between family child care providers and parents. Redleaf Press and the author are not engaged in rendering legal, accounting, or other professional services. If legal or expert assistance is required, the reader should consult the services of a qualified professional. All names used in this book are fictitious.

© 1991, 1997 by Tom Copeland
All rights reserved. First edition 1991
Second edition 1997
Printed in the United States of America

Published by
Redleaf Press
a division of Resources for Child Caring
450 North Syndicate, Suite 5
St. Paul, Minnesota 55104

Library of Congress Cataloging-in-Publication Data
Copeland, Tom.
    Family child care contracts & policies: how to be businesslike in a caring profession/Tom Copeland. — 2nd ed.
        p. cm.
    ISBN: 0-934140-70-7 (alk. paper)
    1. Family day care—United States. 2. Family day care—Law and legislation—United States. 3. Contracts—United States.
I. Title.
HQ778.63.C65 1997
362.7′12′0687—dc21   97-5321
                                                           CIP

TABLE OF CONTENTS

Introduction

This book was written to help family child care providers establish and enforce contracts and policies with the parents of the children in their care. A family child care provider is defined in this book as someone who works out of her or his own home caring for one or more children on behalf of the parents. The provider may only be caring for the children of relatives or close friends. The provider may be licensed, regulated, or certified according to local rules, or may be exempt or in violation of these rules. This book is addressed to all such providers. It discusses:

- What to look for before signing a contract with a parent
- What to include in a contract
- What to include in provider policies
- How to prevent conflicts with parents
- How to respond when a parent does not abide by the contract or policies
- When and how to change contract terms and provider policies
- When and how to end the contract

What Is a Contract?

Simply stated, a contract should only deal with the agreement to provide child care and the cost of the care. Everything else should be covered in the provider policies. A contract is a legal, binding agreement between two people involved in an exchange of services. If a provider agrees to care for a child and the parent agrees to pay for that care, a contract has been made. Both parties must expect that the other will follow through on the promises in their agreement. If the terms of the contract are broken, either party is entitled to seek payment for damages. A contract does not have to be in writing, although it is much more difficult to enforce a verbal contract.

What Are Provider Policies?

Provider policies are those rules and behaviors that deal with how the provider will care for the children. Policies usually cover such things as discipline, daily activities, meal schedules, procedures to care for children with special needs, and arrangements in case of illness and other emergencies.

Unlike other publications and sample contracts, this book makes a distinction between a contract and provider policies and recommends that providers do likewise. A provider can change the policies without any notice and the parents' only real recourse is to remove the child from care. If a provider refuses to provide care (or if a parent refuses to pay for the care), the parties are entitled to sue each other for breach of contract. A more detailed explanation of what to include in a contract and provider policies is given in chapters 4 and 5.

I hope that this book will serve as a practical guide for how to use written contracts and provider policies successfully. This book uses two examples of a contract. The first example uses only a few simple terms, while the other is more comprehensive. A new provider, or someone who has never used a written contract before, may be more comfortable starting out with the shorter sample contract. Chapter 5 contains many examples of provider policies and forms. Complete copies of all of these documents can be found in the appendix.

Although this book emphasizes the importance of creating and enforcing formal agreements, it also stresses that contracts and provider policies are not substitutes for communication between parent and provider. In fact, a formal agreement is a communication tool used to clarify the relationship and expectations between a provider and a parent.

You Are in Control

Family child care providers are entitled to set up their own contract and policies however they wish. The only legal constraint is that their rules cannot violate local, state, or federal law. Federal or state laws may prohibit discrimination based on race, color, sex, disability, religion, or national origin. Check your state and local laws for further information. Other than these specific laws, however, providers are virtually free to run their business how they want. In this book I attempt to explain how a contract and policies can be used to make your business run more smoothly. You do not have to agree with everything I say. If you have an arrangement with parents that works for you, that's great. I am not out to change something that doesn't need fixing. I hope you will take from this book what makes sense to you and will work in your community, and leave the rest. It's your decision.

A Word on Language

Throughout this book, the terms "contract" and "agreement" will be used interchangeably. In addition, in order to avoid the awkward use of "he/she" when referring to a parent, the plural ("parents") is often used. Despite the increasing likelihood that a child will only be cared for by one parent, the plural allows the use of the gender-neutral pronoun "them." When it is unavoidable, gender-specific pronouns are used alternately throughout the book.

Statements made in this book about legal agreements should not be considered as official, legal opinion or conclusive determination of the subject. When legal advice is appropriate, providers should consult an attorney. For feedback on local practices, providers should ask the advice of their peers and seek help from provider organizations, Child Care Food Program sponsors, child care resource and referral agencies, or their licensor/regulator.

To help providers better understand some relevant tax rules, brief tax tips have been inserted throughout the book. For a more detailed explanation of record keeping and tax issues, see *The Basic Guide to Family Child Care Record Keeping* and the *Family Child Care Tax Workbook,* both published by Redleaf Press.

Acknowledgments

I want to acknowledge that the work of Margareta Vranicar played an important role in this book. Eileen Nelson, Debbie Hewitt, and Anne Thompson from Resources for Child Caring provided valuable assistance. Readers who offered valuable suggestions include: Diane M. Phillippi, LSW, family day care licensor, Ramsey County; Rose Cerato, field station manager and Lucy Tschogl, Las Vegas Coordinator, America West Airlines Child Care Department; Abbey Cohen, Child Care Law Center; Madeleine Baker, Lincoln National Corporation; Pat Ward, Family Day Care Project, National Council of Jewish Women; Joe Perreault, Save the Children, Atlanta; Diane Adams, Child Care Coordinating Council, Madison, Wisconsin, and family child care providers Debra Goodlaxson, Lynne Coates, Darlene Tonga, and Stephen C. and Deborah A. Dietz. Thanks also to Fredrik Hausmann, Kathy Raskob, Paul Woods, and Judy Gilats for their work on the design and production of this edition.

I would also like to acknowledge the major contribution made by Phyllis Karasov, Esq., of Moore, Costello and Hart, St. Paul, Minnesota.

Finally, I appreciate the many hardworking family child care providers whom I have met and talked with over the years. Their experiences have helped shape this book.

Chapter 1: Being a Professional in a Caring Profession

Anyone can love a child, but it requires skill to properly take care of one. It takes skill to care for a group of children of different ages on a day to day basis over a long period of time. This is the job of today's family child care provider. It is a unique job not duplicated by any other profession.

A family child care provider is a self-employed businessperson who has many responsibilities: caring for children, dealing with parents, managing a business, and caring for her own family. Along with the rewards of running a business, there are also risks involved, such as possible injury to children, damage to property, or being the target of a lawsuit. As every family child care provider knows, this job is not simple.

To be successful, you need to establish and maintain a professional business relationship with the parents of the children in your care, even when the parent is a relative or close friend. You should take yourself and your work seriously and treat parents as business clients. Nothing said in this book should be taken to mean that you have to be rude or unsympathetic in order to deal successfully with parents, however. There is no conflict between being a friendly, caring person and presenting yourself to parents in an organized, businesslike manner.

Dealing with a business client means setting up the rules of your relationship through a contract and policies, following these rules in good faith, and treating parents with respect. This requires keeping a certain emotional distance from parents, which can be hard to do when you are so close to their children. But maintaining a business relationship with parents is necessary for you to best care for the children and be compensated fairly for your

Safe Havens by *Bill Holbrook*

Panel 1: "SUE, I KNOW YOU DON'T WANT TO RAISE THE DAY-CARE CENTER'S RATES, BUT THE ONLY ALTERNATIVE IS TO DECLARE BANKRUPTCY!"

Panel 2: "FOR JUST THIS TIME YOU HAVE TO ABANDON YOUR ROLE AS A NURTURER AND LET YOUR BUSINESS SIDE TAKE OVER!"

Panel 4: "WHAT DO YOU MEAN, CAN YOU BORROW MY SHAVING CREAM?"

© 1991, Washington Post Writers Group. Reprinted with permission.

1

work. When negotiating and enforcing a contract with parents, providers can be tough without being coldhearted. You should strive to stick to your own rules and set your own limits. Being tough also means saying no to unreasonable requests by parents. It is always appropriate for you to use assertive, rather than aggressive, behavior to express your feelings and enforce your agreements. Although you can never please all parents, most parents will come to trust a provider who demonstrates that she has given some careful thought to the rules governing the care of children.

Your own family and friends can be a source of support in your effort to adopt a more professional business attitude. Ask them to give you moral support as you negotiate and enforce your contract and provider policies. Explain to them that by being more businesslike, you are likely to resolve conflicts faster, reduce debts, and obtain greater peace of mind. You can encourage their support by communicating to them the satisfaction you feel as a successful, professional provider.

Family child care providers are successful when they are able to distinguish and find a balance between the caring attention required for child care and the attention required for owning a business. Therefore, a successful provider is someone who:

1) Uses the most appropriate techniques to care for children and to help them reach their potential

2) Meets all local licensing/regulation requirements (whether or not they are voluntary)

3) Continues to increase her knowledge about all aspects of the business by taking regular training workshops, reading professional magazines, joining the Child and Adult Care Food Program, and seeking advanced credentials in the field

4) Works to improve the profession by joining other child care providers in local and national child care associations

5) Conducts her work in a businesslike manner by keeping complete, accurate records, communicating regularly with parents, and filing the proper state and federal tax forms

Chapter 2: Establishing a Business Relationship With Parents

Providers who can spend many happy hours talking and communicating with children sometimes find it hard to do the same with parents. Providers may complain about parents, saying "They take advantage of me," "They are inconsiderate and difficult to deal with," or "They don't respect my business." These kinds of expressions are not uncommon. Parents may also have legitimate complaints about providers. Conflicts with parents is one of the biggest reasons providers leave the child care field. These conflicts are often caused by providers not demonstrating good business skills and not having the adequate tools to communicate with parents on a business level.

Many parents don't treat family child care as a business. This may be because it is a relatively new business. It is probably fair to say that many parents have practically no idea what family child care providers do all day, what the children learn, how providers manage their time, or even how much money providers earn for their long hours of work. Family child care is a new experience for them. In fact, this is the last generation of parents who have little or no firsthand experience of being in a family child care home as a child. Also, parents may not treat family child care as a business because providers often don't act like they are running a business. Establishing a business relationship with parents will open the lines of communication and bring you the respect you deserve.

A family child care provider is a self-employed businessperson. You are not the employee of the parent. You, not the parents, set the rules. Providers are often timid about how they run their business. You can operate a highly structured or loosely structured program. You can serve meals with lots of meat, or serve only vegetarian food. You can care for infants or exclude infants from your program. You can have hundreds of rules that parents must follow or only a few rules. The type of service you offer to parents is strictly up to you. This is the way it works in any business. Just as customers don't tell the bank how to run its business, providers should not allow parents to set rules for them.

Providers should first decide how they will run their business and then let parents know what to expect. This is not an easy task for many providers. There is no one else to set the rules and enforce them; no director, manager, or supervisor. The provider does everything. She is the activity planner, cook, cleaner, rule setter and rule enforcer, bill collector, salesperson, etc. It can be an overwhelming job having to care for children while dealing with business issues. But it will always be the responsibility of providers to establish and maintain a business relationship with parents.

Some providers feel uncomfortable talking with parents about money and rules. Providers grow close to the children they care for and can get involved in the personal lives of the parents as well. This, however, does not relieve the provider of the responsibilities of being a business owner. These responsibilities are not shared with the parents. Some providers try to ignore these responsibilities by treating parents as friends. This is a mistake. Providers are often disappointed when the parents do not return their overtures of friendship. The problem is not with the parents. Parents are looking for child care, not friendship. Providers can choose to have close relationships with parents, but they can never abdicate their role as business owners.

This chapter will not cover the general subject of good communication. There are other books that deal extensively with this (for example, *Working with Difficult People* by Muriel Solomon). Nor will this chapter dwell on the inappropriate behavior of parents. You may not be able to change parents' behavior, but you can improve your own business practices. Stated simply, if you set up reasonable business policies and set limits with parents, you can control what goes on by enforcing your rules and giving notice to those parents who won't follow them.

Of course it is not quite that easy. Having an organized business and a clear contract doesn't necessarily mean you'll be free of problems or setbacks. Parents have a right to complain about the kind of care being given to their child, and providers have a right to expect that their policies will be respected. You can avoid many problems or reduce their consequences by establishing effective communication channels with parents.

The Six Steps to a Successful Business

Step 1: Reduce the risks of doing business

Step 2: Use props to communicate your rules

Step 3: Keep careful records

Step 4: Communicate regularly with parents

Step 5: Make notes as events occur

Step 6: Use a contract and provider policies

Step 1: Reduce the Risks of Doing Business

You must protect yourself and the children in your care by being a risk manager. You need to be able to anticipate the possibility that things can go wrong and take measures to reduce their impact. Although you can never completely eliminate the additional risks you face in your business, you can reduce these risks by following sound business management practices. It is important for you to communicate to parents your role as a risk manager. This will demonstrate that you recognize your business responsibilities and are serious about protecting the children. Because they will better understand the steps you have taken to reduce the risks for their children, it will also reduce the likelihood that parents will sue.

Here are six ways to reduce the risks of doing business:

1) Conduct a regular safety inspection of your home to reduce the risk of accidents. You may need to make changes to operate in accordance with state or local licensing and building code rules. Tell parents what has been done to make your home safe. Ask parents for suggestions about what else might be done. When appropriate, review the house rules and safety procedures with the children to help them understand how to avoid dangers. Be firm about what types of behavior are and are not allowed that relate to home safety.

2) Develop a policy that describes how you will handle emergencies such as fires, earthquakes, tornadoes, and accidents. Take a course in first aid and CPR (cardiopulmonary resuscitation). Have emergency phone numbers on hand for the doctor, police, hospital, poison control center, backup caregivers, and parents. Show parents where you keep your emergency numbers and give them a copy of your emergency policies. Bring emergency information and first aid supplies with you when you go on field trips.

3) Review your insurance policies to make sure your business is covered in these areas:

   a) Vehicle insurance: To cover injuries to you and your assistants, the children in your care, and damages to your car while it is being used for business purposes.

   b) Disability insurance: To cover loss of income if you cannot work. You can get short- and long-term disability insurance.

   c) Accident/Medical insurance: To cover doctor, emergency room, and hospital bills resulting from injuries to you or your own children that occur at your home or on field trips.

   d) Homeowner's insurance: To cover damage to your home and to protect yourself if someone is injured on your property. Note that homeowner's insurance usually limits coverage for any business property damaged or destroyed by such disasters as fires, floods, or tornadoes. Providers should see if their swing sets, bikes, toys, and other business equipment is covered. If not, purchase additional insurance coverage.

   e) Liability insurance: To cover the risk of accidents, claims of slander, and claims of negligence. Liability insurance also protects you in the event of certain types of lawsuits.

   f) Personal property insurance: To cover damage to, or loss of, household furniture, appliances, and play equipment.

   g) Umbrella insurance policy: To cover your home, auto, and liability insurance. This kind of package may provide more coverage at a lower rate than separate policies.

Discuss insurance with parents and ask them about their insurance coverage. Some states have specific laws requiring providers to carry certain types of insurance. Often parents' personal insurance policies provide some protection for their own children. Consider charging parents an extra fee for any additional business, medical, car, or property insurance you obtain. It is a business expense that will also protect the parents and their children. Some providers have parents sign a waiver that says parents won't sue them in the event of an accident or injury to their child. Such waivers are of little protection in court unless they are carefully written. Use a lawyer to draft such a waiver.

4) Comply with all child care licensing or registration requirements that will help ensure the maintenance of a healthy and safe environment for children. In some states, providers can't get insurance unless they are operating legally. Tell parents what it means to be licensed or registered. It is strongly recommended that you follow the most comprehensive local rules concerning licensing/registration, even when compliance is voluntary. Following such rules provides additional protection for you, the children in your care, and their parents. It is also an important sign of professionalism.

5) Screen and closely supervise anyone hired to help care for children, even if it is only on a very temporary basis. Tell parents how assistants are chosen.

6) Report suspected incidents of child abuse or neglect to the proper local authorities. You should educate yourself about what to look for and share this information with parents. Some states require providers to report suspected child neglect or abuse. If this is the case, you should inform parents of your responsibility.

Step 2: Use Props to Communicate Your Rules

It is difficult for many providers to talk directly with parents about money or other business matters. Providers who want to be firm in their communications with parents might want to use written materials or props. Physical props can be a helpful way to create a more formal, businesslike atmosphere with parents. Here are some examples:

1) Bills and receipts: Give parents a bill or invoice that tells them how much money they owe. Pass out a receipt when they pay you. Giving a written bill or offering to give a parent a receipt is often easier than verbally asking for money.

2) Pay boxes: Establish an official place where you store parent payments. Some providers put out a cigar box on the day payments are due. Affix a sign to the box that says "Place payments here." Parents are thus reminded to deposit their money in the box without the provider having to say anything.

3) Newsletters: Providers can use a monthly newsletter to announce new rules or remind parents of current policies. These announcements may include rate increases, reminders to sign special permission forms, notices of special events, or menus.

4) Bulletin boards: Providers can post business and nonbusiness announcements on bulletin boards to keep parents informed.

5) Home videos: Some providers videotape special parties or activities and offer to loan the tape to parents so they can watch it with their children. Children love seeing themselves on TV and it sends the message that you are a busy, professional caregiver.

Step 3: Keep Careful Records

To run a well-managed business you need to keep good business records. You will need to keep track of all business income and expenses in order to file your tax returns. Some states even require providers to keep certain records on file. In general, you will need to keep written records such as parent contracts, provider policies, parent enrollment forms, children's medical records, field trip and medical authorization forms, receipts for payments, attendance records, and any documents dealing with the Child and Adult Care Food Program. Sample copies of most of these forms can be found in the appendix.

$ *Tax Note: All business records necessary to complete federal tax forms must be kept for three years after the tax form has been filed. To be safe, save them for four years. Keep receipts and invoices of any major home improvements or equipment purchases (such as swing sets, furniture, and appliances) for as long as you are depreciating them in your business, plus an additional three years.*

Having organized records will make it easier for you to conduct business with parents. Records can also be used to help providers better understand their own business.

Step 4: Communicate Regularly with Parents

You should get into the habit of communicating with parents in a variety of ways and on a regular basis. Having a written contract and provider policies is only one way of communicating. The parent interview is an opportune time to discuss the value of regular communication. At this time you might announce your policy of communicating with parents at the end of each day to let them know about their child's day. It will be easier to discuss problems if the habit of sharing with each other has been established early. If the parent is too rushed to be able to talk when the child is dropped off or picked up, perhaps exchanging short written notes will keep each other informed. If necessary, use the phone during the evening. If a daily schedule of talks or notes seems too much, try it on a weekly basis.

Try to establish a consistent pattern of dialogue and stick to it. It is a good idea to regularly schedule time alone with a parent—at least every three months—to discuss how the child is doing and how the business arrangement is working. Establish regular communication patterns with both parents of a child, if both have custody. Parents do not always see things the same way, so providers should be talking to both. If you can't get together with the parents this often, try to schedule it every six months or when the contract is normally reviewed. The business discussion could be very simple: "Things are running smoothly, Peter. I appreciated your willingness to bring an extra set of clothes for our field trip last week and I thank you for picking up Anna on time, even though I know you have a tight schedule. How has our arrangement been working for you?"

Or the conversation might be more involved: "Most things are working well between us, Latitia, but we do have one problem. You know our contract calls for you to pay me each Monday morning, and last week I didn't get paid until Wednesday. It is a problem for me, even when you pay me on Monday evening, because I need the money to cover some bills I pay that day. I can't be flexible about this part of our contract. What can we do to correct this?"

The next chapter explains how to deal with contract violations. The point here is that having a regular meeting time can give providers the opportunity to discuss problems with parents before too much time has passed. It is always better to notify parents quickly when problems arise rather than to wait, only to suddenly surprise them with a litany of complaints.

❓ Question: Abusive Language

"What do I do about a parent who treats me with disrespect and uses abusive language around the children? I provide wonderful care for his child and I'd hate to see the child leave."

Answer: Outside of the children's hearing, say to the parent, "I won't allow you to use that kind of language around these children. If you do so again, I will ask you to leave the room immediately." Specifically describe the behavior that offends you ("I do not appreciate it when you...") and the action you are requesting ("I want you to stop..."). No matter how much you care about a child, it is not healthy for you to accept discourteous treatment from a parent. Insist on being treated with respect. If you don't get it, end the relationship.

Parent Evaluations

Providers should consider giving parents the opportunity to write a written evaluation once a year or when they decide to withdraw their child from care. Even parents who are leaving may have some useful ideas or comments. Such an evaluation can be simple and might look like this:

Parent Evaluation Form

1) *What do you like best about how your provider cares for your child?*

   (Sample answers)

   "I love the way you give Keisha a warm welcome and a big hug each morning."

   "Henry is always talking about how many fun activities he does in day care, especially playing outside in your yard."

2) *What do you wish your provider would do differently about caring for your child?*

   (Sample answers)

   "Nothing much. I sometimes wish Mike wasn't so dirty when I come to pick him up."

   "I wish your policy was more flexible about caring for my child after 6:00 P.M. Sometimes it is a real problem leaving work to get there by then."

3) *What else can you suggest that would help your provider do a better job?*

   (Sample answers)

   "Can you keep Larry inside when the other kids play outside?"

   "I would appreciate knowing Sunday night that another child has been exposed to measles, not Monday morning."

4) *What actions might you take that would help improve the care your child receives here?*

   (Sample answers)

   "I will try to remember to bring enough diapers at the beginning of the week so you don't run out."

   "If it would help, I can bring some of John's toys that he's outgrown for the other children to play with."

5) *Would you recommend your provider to other parents? Why or why not?*

   (Sample answers)

   "Yes, I am very satisfied with the care my child receives."

   "No, I am leaving because the house is too dirty and cluttered."

6) *Other Comments:*

   (Sample comments)

   "There doesn't seem to be enough books and toys for my six year old."

   "I particularly like the singing games you share with my children. Thank you!"

Parent's name (optional) _____ Date _____

Child's name (optional) _____

After the parent completes the evaluation, review the comments and discuss the issues raised. If the comments are favorable, you may want to ask the parent if you can use the evaluation as a reference for prospective clients. You might ask your licensor/regulator for additional feedback. They may offer suggestions for improvement.

How should you deal with negative evaluations? First of all, you should understand that you will never be able to please everyone. You should thank parents for their feedback and then think before responding directly to criticism. If the complaint is vague ("I don't like my child's daily schedule"), ask for clarification ("What would you like your child to be doing differently?"). If the complaint comes from only one parent, you might get a better perspective by asking the other parents if they experience the same problem.

Some complaints may be valid, some may not. If you believe the complaint is valid ("Your house is too dirty"), you should take steps to change things ("I will make an effort to clean more before the children arrive in the morning"). If you believe the complaint is not valid ("I wish you were more flexible about caring for Sandy after 6 P.M."), you should make it clear that things will not change ("I'm sorry you are unhappy with my policy, but I'm unwilling to care for any children beyond 6 P.M., the time spelled out in our agreement"). You can use parent criticism as an opportunity to identify and correct minor problems before they become major ones that might threaten the relationship.

Step 5: Make Notes As Events Occur

Most problems with parents do not arise out of the blue. They usually begin with small incidents that are not resolved. To head off many conflicts, it is a good idea for you to start a policy of writing a short note every time an incident occurs. The notes don't always have to be about problems. You might also write a note to remember a time when a child or a parent did something positive. Keep a file of notes for each family.

Let's look at an example to see how taking notes can be useful. One day Charlie bites another child. You write a note in your records that says:

> May 12 - Charlie bit Denise without warning

That evening you talk to Charlie's father. Neither of you can offer an explanation for why the incident happened. You decide to keep more detailed records. After two weeks this is what you have recorded:

Notes on Charlie Baldwin

May 12 - Charlie bit Denise without warning
May 14 - Charlie bit Nancy at noon and 4pm
May 15 - Charlie bit Denise during an argument,
        another biting at noon with no reason.
May 19 - Charlie bit Denise fighting over Big Wheel
May 21 - Charlie bit Denise at 11:30am
May 22 - Charlie bit Denise at 12:15pm
May 26 - Charlie bit Nancy at 4:30pm

After two weeks you and Charlie's father sit down to talk. After reviewing the notes, it appears that Charlie bites Denise more than any other child. Why? Maybe the two should be kept apart more. Also, Charlie seems to be biting most around noon. Is he tired? Would an earlier lunch help? Is he biting because he's not getting his way? How can this be resolved?

After your discussion, write down any decisions you and the parent make regarding what is to be done. Both you and the parent can use the records to help understand what is happening to Charlie. You may want to try changing some things and record whether it makes any difference. Without such notes, it may be harder to pinpoint when the biting occurs or who is bitten the most. If the problem is serious enough to warrant seeking professional help, the notes documenting the behavior may result in faster treatment. When you keep short written notes, you can promote better communication with parents and enhance the quality of care for the children.

$ *Tax Note: Keeping careful records can also help reduce your taxes. Keep track of the hours you spend in meetings and phone conversations with parents, doing parent interviews, and writing notes. If you are spending this time when the children you care for are not present, you may count these hours in your Time-Space calculation for tax purposes. It is to your financial benefit to keep track of all the time you spend in your home on business activities.*

Step 6: Use a Contract and Provider Policies

A contract and provider policies are two vital tools of business communication, but they should not be viewed as the only means by which providers and parents communicate. The five steps above describe communication techniques which are equally valuable. While much of the rest of this book will discuss the technical aspects of establishing and enforcing a contract and provider policies, you should not forget that the primary purpose of having a contract and provider policies is to facilitate communication. Very few contract disputes ever wind up in a court of law. Although it is important to pay attention to the legal issues surrounding the signing of a contract, the most practical reason for developing a contract and provider policies is so both parties can better understand what is expected of them. If both parties sign these documents but never looked at them again, they were not very useful. Contracts, and particularly provider policies, should be seen as living documents that can be changed to reflect new circumstances and expectations.

After taking the steps to develop better business communication skills, you are ready to enter into a written agreement.

? Question: Getting Started with a Contract

"I've been a child care provider for a long time but I've never used a contract. How do I begin using one?"

Answer: You can start using a contract with parents at any time. Draw up a contract (or use a sample one that is available) and sit down with each parent to discuss it. Tell them at least two weeks in advance that you want to begin operating under a written agreement. Parents may say, "We've gotten along just fine so far, why do we need a contract? Don't you trust me?" You can reply, "I want to use a contract so we can more easily remember our verbal agreements and to help us resolve any differences we might have. I think it is a good idea to put down our expectations of each other and review them from time to time to make sure things are running smoothly." Insist on a deadline by which the parents must sign the contract. If they refuse, discontinue providing them with child care.

Chapter 3:   Establishing a Contract

What to Look For Before Signing a Contract

No provider should feel obligated to care for the children of everyone who asks. Many providers who later have a conflict with a parent will say, "I knew this person was trouble right from the start. I could tell we were going to have problems." If you feel uneasy about the parent right away, you should not be afraid to turn the parent down. It may be better to resist the urge to care for a child if you know the relationship won't last. In this situation it will probably also be better for the child not to be changing providers.

The best time to look for signs that an agreement should not be made with someone is during the interview. Set aside enough time to go over the details of your business, including all the terms of the contract and the provider policies. You should explain how you deal with issues such as discipline, toilet learning, and naps. Clearly express your philosophy about caring for children. You should use this opportunity to sell yourself by pointing out your strengths (years of experience, educational background, special training or equipment, varied activity schedule, comfortable indoor or outdoor play areas, and so on). Invite the parent to bring the child along for the interview.

Describe your expectations of parents. You should ask parents if they understand everything you are saying. Ask them about their parenting philosophy. What do the parents think of the contract and provider policies? How does the parents' approach to raising children differ from yours? Have the parents used other providers in the past, and if so, what kinds of problems did they have? If the parents don't feel comfortable with some of the terms in your contract, ask them to take the contract home and think about it. Never rush into signing anything.

If you are licensed/regulated, show parents the license. Discuss what is and is not covered by the license or certification with regard to the child's safety, health, and daily activities. Offer a tour of your facilities, including bathrooms, toys, equipment, and the areas where the children nap, play, and eat. Introduce the new child to your family and the other children in your care. Talk about your family's routine and activities and how they will affect the children in your care. If you must begin cooking dinner for your own family by 5:00 P.M., or if your daughter must be driven to band practice at 4:30, the parents should be told this to explain why the 4:15 pick up time is important.

As you are getting to know the parents and child during the interview, look for these warning signs that may indicate it is not a good idea to establish an agreement:

1) Were the parents unreasonably late for the interview? It may be suggestive of things to come.

2) If the parents have different values than you, can everybody be respectful of one another's views and be comfortable talking about them? Someone who has trouble handling conflict may later decide to just leave rather than work out a problem.

3) Do the parents show an interest in how you will be caring for their child? If not, you may later become frustrated trying to involve them in addressing the child's needs.

4) Do the parents show a willingness to be flexible and to compromise? If not, you may have trouble handling unforeseen problems.

5) Observe the parents' child. Are there signs that indicate providing care for this child would be unreasonably difficult?

6) Let the child play with the other children in your home. If the child climbs all over the furniture, does this bother you? Do the parents object to your telling the child not to climb on the furniture? Some habits may be hard to break.

7) Lastly, do the parents treat you with respect and have a positive attitude about your ability to care for children? Stay away from self-centered people who are inconsiderate of you and your profession.

You should trust your feelings about parents. If parents are difficult to deal with during the interview, chances are things won't be any easier later on. If the parents don't respect your professional way of doing business, it is probably best not to enter into a working relationship with them.

© 1991, Washington Post Writers Group. Reprinted with permission.

References

Many parents ask providers for references before making a decision to enroll their child. Parents want to learn more about the provider. Is the provider a reliable, responsible, caring person? The request for references is reasonable and providers should have several names available upon request. The best references are parents whose children were in your care for many years. When parents leave, ask if they would be willing to be a reference for you.

Although it may seem awkward at first, providers should also ask parents for references. Ask the parents for the name(s) of the previous caregivers of their child. You are about to make an important decision to spend ten or more hours a day with a child. It is not unreasonable to want to know more about the parents and the child. If a parent refuses to give you a reference, use your own judgment to determine if the parent's explanation is reasonable. You are unlikely to be able to get a reference from a parent who has an infant. Also, parents may be reluctant to give out the name of their current provider if they haven't told the person they are leaving.

Once you have the names of one or two references, call the references and ask four basic questions:

1) How long did you care for the child?

2) Were there any problems you had with the child or parents that I should know about?

3) What are some of the positive things you can tell me about the child and the parents?

4) If given the opportunity, would you provide care for this child again?

The last question is probably the most important one. You are looking for any major problems that might affect your relationship with the child or parent. Don't worry about minor past conflicts, such as the parents arriving late to pick up their child once in eight months, or the child crying for an hour several times after the parents have left. Major problems might include the parent leaving while owing money to the previous provider, or the child being sick every other week because the parent wouldn't take the child to a doctor. Listen closely to what the reference tells you, but remember that people respond differently to conflict. What upsets one person may not bother you.

Slander

What if a provider calls you for a reference on one of your previous clients. Should you worry that your comments could get you in trouble? If you falsely say something that would cause their reputation in the community to be damaged, you have committed slander and could be sued for damages. If what you say about your previous client can be proved, however, you have a sound defense against a slander lawsuit. For example, telling the provider who calls you that the parent's payment was late seven times in four months is a statement that can be proved. Your defense against a slander lawsuit is compromised when you make statements that can't be proved, such as "The person always paid late." Stick to the facts in any statement you give to another provider. For example, "The child cried for an hour in the morning, three times a week," "The parent left owing me $250," or "The parent was verbally abusive to me on two occasions last July." Parents will rarely sue for slander. Don't create unnecessary trouble for yourself by criticizing past clients with broad accusations.

How to Say No to a Parent

At the beginning of the parent interview you should make it clear that both you and the parent have to agree to the caregiving arrangement. Some parents think that you will automatically consent to care for their child. Tell the parent, "Before enrolling your child, we both need to agree to the decision." It should not be a surprise to the parent that you may not want to take their child.

If you refuse to enroll a child, use neutral language that does not blame the child or the parent. If you say something directly negative ("I don't trust that you will pay me on time," or "I don't think your child will be accepted by my other children"), you are likely to offend the parent more than necessary. A parent who feels ill-treated is more likely to say something bad about you or your program to another prospective client. The parent may ask for specific reasons, but you should not elaborate. If you must say more, tell the parent, "It's not personal. I try to make my decision based on what is best for your child. My feelings tell me that your child would be better cared for by someone else."

It can be hard to say no to a parent. But your decision should be based on what is best for you, your business, your family, and the other children in your care, as well as what is best for the new child. It is better to say no than to accept the child and then give the parent notice six months later because of a conflict that couldn't be resolved.

Some providers accept children on a trial basis, quite often lasting two weeks. A written contract may allow that during this time either party may end the arrangement without any notice. It gives both sides a chance to back out gracefully if problems arise. If you choose to adopt such a trial period, observe how things are going and discuss any problems at the end of the period. If you have completed the interview process to your satisfaction, you are ready to think about establishing a contract.

When is it Okay to Discriminate Against a Parent and/or a Child?

Providers should be aware of when it is illegal to discriminate against a parent or child. Federal law may prohibit you from denying care to a child because of race, color, sex, disability, religion, or national origin. Check your state and local laws to see if there are additional prohibitions. The laws concerning discrimination against people with disabilities was greatly expanded in 1992 with the passage of the Americans with Disabilities Act (ADA). The ADA essentially states that you have to make "reasonable accommodation" for a child with a disability. "Reasonable accommodation" is a subjective phrase. Among the things the law takes into account are the burden and the expense the requested accommodation would require. You do not have to implement the requested accommodation if doing so would create a significant difficulty or expense for you. All family child care providers are required to follow the rules of the ADA. For further information on discrimination issues contact the Child Care Law Center (see appendix for address), or your child care resource and referral agency.

Other than the specific laws against discrimination cited in the previous paragraph, you may choose to provide or terminate care for a variety of reasons. You can stop care because the parents are always late with their payment, they bounced a check, they made a false complaint against you to your licensing worker, or simply because you don't feel like caring for their child anymore. Age discrimination laws only apply to adults, so you can refuse to care for a child based on age. You don't need a reason to refuse to enroll a child, nor do you need one to terminate your contract with a parent. It is better not to lie about why you are refusing to enroll a child (claiming your program is full, for example). If the parents learn about the lie, they may believe that you discriminated against them and sue you. Without identifying any specific reason, simply tell the parents you aren't accepting their child. See chapter 6 for more information on how to terminate care.

Many providers may be reluctant to establish firm rules about their business and to put their agreement with parents in writing. They may feel that it is easier to start out on an informal basis and keep everything casual as long as things are going well. There could be several reasons for providers to take this position. They may not be sure of what to expect of parents or themselves, they could be eager to build their reputation, or they could be so eager to please parents that they will enroll children at all costs. Other providers may be afraid of alienating or losing parents by creating a more formal relationship. Some providers might even feel that a written agreement is at odds with the main purpose of caring for children.

A growing number of providers in recent years, however, are convinced that written contracts and provider policies are a necessary part of doing business. Many parents, in fact, welcome written agreements. The use of a written agreement is viewed as a sign that a provider is organized, responsible, and easy to communicate with. A provider with thought-out written policies can use them as a selling point to attract some parents.

A written contract serves many purposes:

1) It makes both parties aware that they are entering into a serious, formal agreement that is to be honored.

2) It can be used to remind both parties of what they promised to do.

3) It can help resolve conflicts by explaining the consequences of violating the contract.

4) It can be used by the provider or parent to support her case against the other in a lawsuit.

Written provider policies also serve many purposes:

1) They force both parties to take steps to help protect the health and safety of the child by planning ahead for emergencies.

2) They describe the procedures used, thereby clarifying the expectations of both parties and reducing parents' anxiety about leaving their child with the provider.

3) They help the provider to be organized and to offer more consistent, reliable care.

Verbal Contracts

One afternoon Juanita and Sandy are discussing child care. When Juanita agrees to pay Sandy $75 a week to care for her child, a verbal contract has been made. Although it is strongly recommend that you use a written contract, a contract does not have to be in writing to be enforceable in court. The principal drawback of a verbal contract is that it can be terminated immediately by either party. Often this can mean that the provider loses a paying customer without warning.

Verbal contracts usually work only in situations where the provider and the parent are in complete agreement about everything at all times. This is nearly impossible, however. For example, how will Sandy deal with the following situations:

1) Juanita's child is sick and stays home for one day. Does Juanita pay Sandy a full $75 for that week?

2) One day Juanita doesn't pick up her child until 7:30 p.m., two hours later than usual. How much does she owe Sandy for that week?

3) The first week, Juanita pays Sandy on Monday, the second week on Wednesday, and the third week on Friday. If Sandy wants to be paid each Monday, what can she do?

Enforcing a verbal contract can be very difficult. Let's say that in the example above, Juanita will not agree to pay for any of the days her child is sick. Sandy had expected to receive $75 a week, no matter how many days the child came. After arguing about it they still don't agree. Sandy could take the case to a small-claims court (sometimes called conciliation court). She could tell the judge that Juanita owes her for sick days because that is what she understood when she agreed to care for Juanita's child. Who will win? The judge must decide what the mutual understanding was when the verbal agreement was made. The party bringing the lawsuit has the burden of proof; that is, to prove that there was mutual agreement in their verbal contract. This would be nearly impossible for Sandy to do and the judge would probably rule against her.

Consider how things would be different if they had a written contract that put their understanding in writing. After talking about it, Sandy and Juanita might have agreed to something like this:

> "The usual weekly rate will be charged for one or two days of illness per week. For more than two days of illness per week the fee will be reduced by $10 for each day missed."

It should be emphasized that Sandy and Juanita could agree to a number of alternate solutions, such as no fee due for any sick days. By clarifying this issue in writing, it is unlikely that Sandy and Juanita would ever have to go to court. If they did, it would probably be very clear (using the example in the box above) that Juanita owes Sandy payment, even if her child is sick for longer than two days a week.

? Question: Unnotified Absences

"A parent didn't bring his child one day last week and didn't call to tell me. The parent doesn't want to pay for that day. What should I tell him?"

Answer: Tell the parent that you were worried when the child didn't show up and that you need to know about absences ahead of time to better plan your day. If your contract doesn't cover this problem, you probably can't ask for payment unless you've agreed earlier that the parent would pay in this situation. Make a written amendment to your contract that will require the parent to pay for absences. After both parties sign the amendment, date it and give the parent a copy. Give the parent notice (two weeks, perhaps) that you are implementing this new policy.

Unregulated Providers and Contracts

It is recommended that all providers abide by the local licensing rules. In fact, all caregivers should meet all local registration rules, even if voluntary. But if you do not comply, you can still use a written contract for all of the purposes described in this chapter. When it comes time to enforce your contract in court, however, you may have a problem. If you misled parents into believing that you were licensed or registered, a judge will likely rule against you. If you are not in compliance with local regulations and have informed the parents of this as soon as you entered into an agreement with them, then it probably won't hurt you in court. Being exempt from local regulations cannot hurt you in court either, unless you misled parents about having a license. A written contract and provider policies offer the same benefits to exempt and illegal providers who disclose this fact to parents as they do to licensed or regulated providers.

$ **Tax Note:** *Parents using an illegal child care provider who cares for more than six children cannot claim the dependent care tax credit for their children in care. An illegal provider is defined as someone who does not meet local licensing requirements. A provider who is exempt from local licensing regulations or who does not comply with a voluntary registration system is not an illegal provider. Parents who use a provider who cares for fewer than six children, whether or not the provider is illegal, are not affected by this tax rule.*

Chapter 4:   What Should Be Included in a Contract

Contracts vs. Provider Policies

There is a significant difference between what should be included in a parent-provider contract and what belongs in provider policies. Most family child care agreements lump the two together, and this can create problems for both parents and providers. Terms that belong in a contract are enforceable by a court, while those matters that belong in provider policies usually are not enforceable by a court. This chapter will focus on what should be included in a contract, and the next chapter covers what belongs in provider policies.

A contract should contain those terms that deal with the parents and the provider's legal rights that can be enforced by a court of law. The most important of these rights are the rights of a provider to be paid for child care, and the rights of a parent to be compensated if the provider fails to deliver the care. In other words, if the provider suddenly refuses to continue caring for a child one day, in violation of the contract that requires the provider to give a two-week notice, the parent can sue the provider for damages (that is, the costs associated with finding a new provider). The provider, in turn, can sue the parent for nonpayment of a fee.

Provider policies usually are not enforceable by a court. For example, if a parent fails to bring an extra change of clothing as required, the provider is not likely to sue the parent for money damages. Likewise, if the provider fails to serve lunch to the children one day, the parent will have difficulty winning a financial judgment against the provider. In both cases, if the two parties can't work out the problem, the usual last resort for either one is to end the relationship.

Combining contract terms and provider policies in one written document limits your flexibility to respond to the changing needs of the parent and child. Provider policies that are drawn up separately from a contract can be changed whenever the provider wishes, based on new circumstances and changes in the needs of one or more of the children. The terms that belong in a contract are meant to be more long-lasting and binding. Neither party can change the contract terms without the agreement of the other. If the details regarding policies such as nap times, daily schedules, and the enforcement of discipline are written as fixed terms of the contract, they are likely to become more rigid and confining as time passes. This will work against the best interests of the children.

There is no one "magic" contract that will meet everyone's needs. Your contract can be short or lengthy. It does not have to be typed, although it would be easier to read. There are a number of sample contracts circulating among providers across the country. Local licensors/regulators may distribute a sample contract. Many providers develop their own after looking over some samples. A sample contract can be useful as long as you make sure it covers all the terms you want to include. Don't be reluctant to change words or entire portions of a sample contract to fit your needs. If you want further help in writing or reviewing a contract, you may want to seek the help of an attorney. See chapter 7 for information about how to choose an attorney.

Four Key Elements to a Contract

There are four key elements that should be included in every written contract:

1) Identification of the child and parent(s)/guardian(s)

2) Payment information

3) Termination procedure

4) Signatures of both parent(s)/guardian(s) and provider

Sample Contracts

If you haven't used a contract before, or if you're just starting out in business, you may want to keep your agreement with parents as simple as possible. To the right is an example of a very basic contract that contains all four key elements. A blank copy of the contract is provided in the appendix.

Although short on details, this brief contract can be used effectively to formalize the business relationship between parent and provider. A new provider, or someone who is just starting to consider using a contract, may be more comfortable with this short contract. You should keep the original signed contract and give a copy to the parents.

Notice that this sample contract allows the provider to end the relationship without giving a two-week notice if a parent fails to make payments on time. Without this contract term, a provider who isn't getting paid would be obligated to give a two-week notice and possibly not collect payment for those two weeks as well. Making reference to the provider policies in the contract notifies the parent that they must abide by them. The provider, however, has the flexibility to change the policies at any time.

Following the basic contract is a sample contract that contains more detail. Notice how even this more complex contract is only an elaboration of the four key elements described above. A blank copy of the contract is provided in the appendix.

Sample Contract #1

1. This contract is made between the Parent(s)/Guardian(s) and Provider for the care of _Rajean_, (name of child) at the home of the Provider.

2. The payment fee shall be: $ _85_ per week / hour
   Payment shall be due on _Monday morning for that week_.

3. This contract may be terminated by either Parent(s)/Guardian(s) or Provider by giving a _2_-week written notice in advance of the ending date. The Provider may immediately terminate the contract without giving any notice if the Parent(s)/Guardian(s) do not make payments when due.

4. The signature of the Parent(s)/Guardian(s) to this contract also indicates that they agree to abide by the written policies of the Provider. The Provider may change these written policies from time to time.

Frances Blackwell   _Cyrus Blackwell_
Mother/Guardian   Father/Guardian

1428 18th Ave N   _225-1067_
Home Address   Home phone

_640-8913_   _252-6800_
Business Phone   Business Phone

Alice Parker   _1/1/97_
Provider   Date Contract Signed

Sample Contract #2

Provider–Parent/Guardian Child Care Agreement

1. The following agreement is made between:

1. _Maria Hernandez-Mayer_   555-1930   641-1241
   Mother/Legal Guardian   Home Phone   Work Phone
   2654 Sherwood Ave., St. Paul, MN 55104
   Home Address
   Law Offices, Snelling Bldg., Suite 600, St. Paul, MN 55161
   Employer's Name and Address

and

2. _Tom Mayer_   555-1930   788-1452
   Father/Legal Guardian   Home Phone   Work Phone
   2654 Sherwood Ave., St. Paul, MN 55104
   Home Address
   Northland Electric, 712 W. 7th St., St. Paul, MN 56143
   Employer's Name and Address

and

3. _Lynn Wymann_   541-3252
   Child Care Provider   Phone
   3624 Clearwood Ave., St. Paul, MN 55104
   Address

for the care of:

4. _Danielle Mayer 6/8/97_ : _____ ;
   Child's Name/Date of Birth   Child's Name/Date of Birth
   Joseph Mayer 4/16/96 : _____ .
   Child's Name/Date of Birth   Child's Name/Date of Birth

2. Basic Rates and Payment Policies:

The payment fee shall be $_180_ per week or $_____ per day or $_____ per hour.

Care shall be provided normally from _7:00_ a.m. to _5:00_ p.m. on these days: (Circle all that apply)

(Monday) (Tuesday) (Wednesday) (Thursday) (Friday) Saturday Sunday.

Additional Fees: _(Fee includes $100/wk for Danielle and $80/wk for Joseph)_

Payment shall be due on: _each Monday morning for the coming week_

3. Overtime Rates:

1. For the purpose of this agreement, overtime will be considered as drop-off before _6:45_ a.m. _____ p.m. and pick-up after _____ a.m. _5:15_ p.m.

2. If the parent/legal guardian makes prior arrangements with the provider, the child may stay overtime at the following rate: $_3.00_ per _15 minutes_ or portion thereof.

3. If the parent/legal guardian has not informed the provider that he or she will be arriving earlier or later than the agreed upon times, the following rate will be charged: $_5.00_ per _15 minutes_ or portion thereof.

© 1991 Redleaf Press

Sample Contract #2

4. Rates Regarding Holidays, Vacations and Other Absences:

1. The following are paid holidays when they fall on a day regularly scheduled for care: *New Year's Day President's Day, Memorial Day, 4th of July, Thksgiving, Xmas*

2. Charges for a child's absence will be: *each child will not be charged for 5 days a year for absences caused by illness or other family emergencies*

3. Charges related to provider's illness or other emergency that prohibit care will be: *no charge*

4. Charges related to provider's scheduled vacation are: *Parents will pay ½ of weekly rate for 2 weeks of provider vacation per year.*

5. Charges related to parent(s)/guardian's scheduled vacation are: *Parents will pay ½ of regular rate for any parent vacations*

   The provider and the parent/guardian will each give **4** weeks advance notice of scheduled vacation or other leave.

6. Other: *In case of emergency absence, parents and provider will notify the other as soon as possible. (see above for charges)*

5. Other Charges:

1. There will be a charge of $ *.60* for each breakfast, $ *1.00* for each lunch, and $ *.35* for each snack served. Other: (OR) *not applicable- provider is in the USDA food program*

2. There will be an extra charge for the following infant supplies when not provided by the parent(s)/legal guardian: *disposable diapers, baby food and formula (based on store prices.)*
   diapers, wipes, baby food, formula, etc.

   and for activity fees/expenses for *swimming lessons and special activities as*
   field trips, children's classes, materials for special projects, etc *agreed in advance.*

3. A holding fee (deposit) of *$180.00* is required to be paid on *1/6/97* which will be applied to the *last* week's payment or forfeited if the child does not come for care as agreed.

6. Termination Procedure:

This contract may be terminated by either parent/guardian or provider by giving **2** weeks written notice in advance of the ending date. Payment by parent/guardian is due for the notice period, whether or not the child is brought to the provider for care. The provider may terminate the contract without giving any notice if the parent/guardian does not make payments when due. Failure by the provider to enforce one or more terms of the contract does not waive the right of the provider to enforce any other terms of the contract.

7. Signatures:

By signing this contract, parent(s)/guardian(s) agree to abide by the written policies of the provider. The provider may amend the policies by giving the parent(s)/guardian(s) a copy of the new or changed policies at least **2** weeks before they go into effect.

Provider's signature *Lynn Nymann*   Date *1/2/97*

Mother/Legal Guardian's signature *Maria Hernandez Mayy*   Date *1/3/97*

Father/Legal Guardian's signature *Tom Mayer*   Date *1/3/97*

Co-signer's signature _____ Date _____

If the parent or legal guardian is under age 18, a co-signer must sign this agreement and act as a guarantor to the contract and agree to be bound by all financial terms.

© 1991 Redleaf Press

Notes About Sample Contract #2:
(Numbers correspond to numbered items in the sample contract.)

2. Payment Rate

It is important for the contract to be very clear about the amount of the fee and when it is due. Disputes over money can be minimized if the contract plainly states the parents' responsibility. For instance, the contract should say when payment is due. It is strongly recommend that you have payment in hand before caring for children. Parents might be asked to make their weekly payments on Monday, not Friday. There are several reasons for requesting payment in advance:

a. Consumers are used to paying for most services before they receive them. Renters pay the landlord at the beginning of the month, not the end. Fees for the YWCA, health clubs, and magazine subscriptions are all due before they are received. Most child care centers charge in advance, too.

b. Providers have expenses throughout the week (food, gas, supplies, etc.) and end up subsidizing parents if they wait to collect fees until the end of the week.

c. The provider will lose income if a parent who normally pays at the end of the week walks out with his child in the middle of a week and refuses to pay for the half week of care provided. If there is a dispute about payments, providers are always better off having the money in hand rather than trying to collect from delinquent parents.

$ *Tax Note: If parents leave owing you money (whether for care already provided or for the notice period), you do not record the amount owed as a bad debt on your tax return. Instead, you record only the lower amount you received as income.*

? *Question: Financial Problems*

"George, a single parent, wants to pay me late this month because he's having financial problems. Should I let him do this?"

Answer: You need to use some judgment when dealing with justifications for not paying. Many providers are sympathetic to the financial difficulties of some parents. Giving a parent extra time to pay may be okay on occasion, but you should not get into the habit of carrying debt for longer than a few weeks. Ask the parent to continue paying you something, even if it is only $10 a week, so the debt won't be forgotten. Set deadlines for when repayments will be made and don't be as ready to forgive a parent who doesn't meet the agreed upon schedule. In the end, if the parent can't afford to be paying you for the care you are providing, you should decide either to give away some of your time or end the business relationship.

© 1991, Washington Post Writers Group. Reprinted with permission.

3. Overtime Rates

It can be very frustrating when parents drop off their children early or are late to pick them up. The contract should state that the regular fee covers a specific time during the day and that there is an extra charge for any care provided before or after this time. You may want to give parents a grace period, perhaps fifteen minutes, or no grace period at all. It is not a good idea to say you'll provide care for a certain number of hours each day because a parent may bring the child one hour later in the morning and expect you to care for the child an extra hour in the evening. If you don't want to work overtime very often, set the overtime fee high enough so that it discourages parents from abusing your time. When at all possible, ask parents to pay for overtime charges on the same day they are incurred.

4. Rates Regarding Holidays, Vacations, and Other Absences

You are free to negotiate whatever you want regarding paid time for your holidays and vacations. You need time off to rest, attend conferences and training workshops, spend time with your own family, and be able to return to your work refreshed. All full-time employees in public and private companies get paid holiday and vacation time. You might want to consider charging for some or all federal holidays: New Year's Day, Presidents' Day, Memorial Day, Fourth of July, Labor Day, Thanksgiving Day, Christmas Day, and Martin Luther King, Jr.'s Birthday. Most child care centers charge for major holidays. Your policy might be that when parents get a paid holiday from their employer, you should be paid for the same holiday.

? *Question: Different Rates*

"Can I charge parents different rates?"

Answer: Yes. You can charge some parents more or less than others as long as you don't base the rates on criteria that are illegal: race, color, sex, disability, religion or national origin. For example, the ADA laws specifically prohibit charging parents more to care for a child with a disability. Under some special circumstances the parents could volunteer to pay extra, but you cannot request that they do so. Some providers charge lower rates because of the parents' financial situation. Others give free days or discounts for parents who have a history of paying on time. If you do charge different rates, you should assume that all parents will eventually find out. Therefore, make sure you have a logical reason for your decision in case you have to explain it later.

Provider Vacations

When you work fifty or more hours in a week for a parent, it is only fair that you receive some paid time off. More and more providers are taking vacation time, although most do not charge parents for these days. It is up to each provider to decide whether or not to charge for vacation. If you can't bring yourself to charge for vacation days, consider raising your regular rate to cover for this time. For example, eight federal holidays plus two weeks of vacation equals eighteen days. If there are 260 working days in a year, eighteen days represents seven percent of the total working days ($18 \div 260 = 7\%$). If you normally charge $80 a week for care and raise your rates seven percent, to $85.60 a week, you will receive the same amount of money as you would had you asked for the eighteen days of paid vacation.

Parent Vacations

Providers should see that their contract clearly addresses whether parents must pay for child care when they take a vacation. Remember, there is no standard practice about whether or not to charge for these days. Your agreement could say that if parents get paid for their vacation, then you should get paid. Some providers charge half of their regular fee for up to two weeks of a parent's vacation. Other providers only charge for a parent's vacation after the child has been in their care for six months or a year. You should ask parents to pay any vacation fees before the vacation is taken. Parents should also be asked to give you some notice before a vacation is taken. Four weeks is probably a reasonable time. You should give the same notice to the parent when you take a vacation. If vacations overlap, and parents are required to pay for either their own and/or the provider's vacation, the parents should pay for any overlap time.

Children's Illness

Children are going to be ill and you should not always lose income when it happens. The contract might say that short-term illnesses of one to four days are to be paid by the parent, but payment may be negotiated in the case of longer illnesses. If a child is gone for more than two weeks, you might ask for a holding fee to keep the space open for the child to return. Another way to approach a child's illness is to charge for the full day only if the parent's employer provides sick pay that can be applied to child care. This will dissuade parents who aren't paid for sick days from returning the sick child to your care sooner than advisable. When you are ill, it is common practice not to charge the parent. But remember, you can set whatever terms you want and you are not obligated to follow the examples described in this book.

5. Other Charges

Make sure your contract covers all miscellaneous charges. Are any discounts offered to those who enroll two or more children from the same family? If a child breaks something around the house, does the parent pay for it? One idea might be that the parent pays if the broken item cost more than $10 and is not covered by insurance. If you provide disposable diapers, a diaper service, baby food, or formula, you may want to charge extra. It may be easier to require parents to provide these items. You may want parents to bring a special snack or treat to help you reduce your food expenses. You cannot charge for food that you are being reimbursed for by the USDA Food Program, however. Check with your sponsor for particular rules regarding parents bringing food. The contract should state whether or not special activities such as swimming lessons, ballet lessons, zoo entrance fees, and other events are to be paid for by the parent. Some providers also charge a penalty fee for any payments that are late and pass on to the parent any bank charges for bounced checks.

Deposits

After an agreement is made between a provider and a parent, there is often a gap of time before the care of the child begins. You should consider requiring parents to pay a deposit to reserve the opening. The amount of the deposit can be negotiated and can be applied toward the first week(s) or last week(s) of care provided. Why is this necessary? When you agree to care for a child two weeks from the day the contract is signed, you are giving up the right to permanently enroll another child. Unless the parent is paying you for this benefit they are receiving, you have given up something for nothing. If the parent does not bring the child as agreed, the deposit will help reimburse you for the time and money you lost while keeping the space open.

Another situation in which charging a deposit might be appropriate is when a parent is pregnant and wants to reserve a space in your program six months or so in the future. You may want to charge the parent a certain amount each week to keep a space reserved. In this instance you would probably keep this money and not apply it to the first or last week(s) of care because you have given up the opportunity to permanently take on a child during a lengthy period of time. You could instead tell the parent that you will not charge a deposit for those weeks that you were able to temporarily fill the space with a child.

❓ *Question: Extra Services*

"At least two or three times a month one parent asks me to do little extra services for her: wash her child's clothes, make an early breakfast, or forgive a bounced check. I don't mind doing some services once in awhile, but it's gotten to be too much. How do I handle this?"

Answer: Before being asked again, tell the parent that you aren't performing any more extra services because they were not part of the original agreement. You may want to ask the parent for something extra in return for the next service you provide, such as payment or a new toy. Or you may simply tell the parent that you want to take a break from doing extra services for the next two months and not to ask for anything more until then.

6. Termination Procedure

Both provider and parents should be able to end their agreement in a relatively short period of time. Even without an advance notice of termination, the courts will probably allow parents to end any such service agreement upon short notice. The contract term that is probably violated most often by parents is the notice of termination. Make sure parents understand that giving a notice means they must pay you for the termination period, whether or not they put their child in your care during this period. The notice period should probably be at least two weeks. The purpose of the notice is to give both parties some time to make other arrangements before the care ends. Without such notice, you could lose income while searching for another child. If you forget or decide not to enforce one term in the contract (overtime fees, for example), this should not prevent you from enforcing another term (such as holiday payments).

Your contract should state that you have the right to terminate care without giving any notice when a parent is behind making payments. This could be stated as follows: "The provider may terminate the contract without giving any notice if the parent/guardian does not make payments when due." Without such a clause in the contract, you are required to give a parent the amount of notice identified in the contract, even when a parent owes money.

You should not have to worry about trying to collect from parents who refuse to pay after giving their notice. You can avoid this problem by requiring that they pay a deposit to cover the period of the termination notice. If the deposit covers the cost of care for a certain amount of time, then you do not have to pay the parent any interest on the deposit. In other words, if the current fee is $80 a week and the parent pays a $160 deposit, which is said to pay for the last two weeks of care (regardless of what the weekly fee may be in the future), you wouldn't owe the parent any interest.

When parents give their notice, tell them you are ready to care for the child during the notice period and there is no additional fee, provided they gave you a deposit for the notice period. If the parents don't want to continue bringing their child, you should say that under the terms of the contract, you will be keeping their deposit.

? *Question: Paying in Advance*

"How do you get parents to start paying you in advance when they have been paying you at the end of the week for years?"

Answer: You can make the change on a number of occasions: at the start of the new year, when you review the contract terms, or at your next meeting with the parent. Write out your new policy about paying in advance and amend it to your contract. Or better yet, redo your contract with this new term. Tell the parent: "Helen, I want to change the time when your payment is due. I need the money in advance because I have expenses during the week that I must pay."

There are two ways to implement such a change. Give the parent at least a month's notice of the change. Ask the parent who now pays $90 each Friday to pay an additional amount with each payment until you have an extra week of payment in hand. For example, the parent could increase their weekly payments to $100 for nine weeks. At the end of this time you would have an extra $90. The parent now returns to paying you $90 on Friday, but this amount is really payment for the upcoming week, since you have already collected that week's $90 payment over time.

Another option is to have parents pay you $5, $10, or $15 on Monday and the remaining amount of their weekly payment on Friday. Increase the amount paid on Monday by $5 a week until the full $90 is being paid on this day. If given enough notice and small, weekly increases, almost any parent can afford this type of transition.

7. Signatures of Both Parties

A written contract is not enforceable until both parties have signed it. If both parents or legal guardians have custody, have each of them sign and date the contract. If the parents later separate, prepare a new contract to be signed by the parent with custody. Written contracts may not be enforceable against a minor. If you are entering a contract with a parent who is under the age of eighteen, have another person such as a relative or friend co-sign the contract along with the minor. Clearly state that if the minor does not pay you for the care she has agreed to under the terms of the contract, the co-signer is responsible for this debt.

It is not recommended that you put any ending date in the contract ("This contract expires one year after it is signed," for instance). People can forget about deadlines and you may find yourself in a situation where the contract has expired without anyone realizing it. In that case, the parent could leave without giving any notice. The parent would not be able to avoid paying for the care you provided, however, even without a written contract.

Partners and Assistants

If two providers are working together as partners, they should sign separate contracts with each parent. If both partners sign the same document with a parent, there is a good possibility that there could be some confusion about lines of communication and responsibility. If one provider is working under the direction of another provider, then only the one in charge should sign the contract. Providers who use assistants should disclose this fact to parents. This could be done by making an addition to the provider policies that states the conditions an assistant may be left alone with the children. Clarify that the parent and provider should communicate directly with each other whenever possible, rather than through the assistant, to reduce the chances of misunderstanding.

? *Question: Getting Paid on Time*

"Sometimes parents will not pay me on time because they forget their checkbooks. What can I do about this?"

Answer: Ask each parent to give you a blank check—no date, name, or signature on it. Put the blank checks in a safe place. The next time a parent forgets her checkbook, pull out the blank check and have her use it. You may want to offer parents the option of leaving a book of blank checks with you out of which they pay each time. This way the parent never has to worry about bringing the checkbook. Remember to give parents a receipt every time they use a blank check so they can balance their checkbook at home. Make sure you put all blank checks in a very secure place. If they are stolen, you may be held responsible for the loss.

In Conclusion

Whether they are stated in a simple or complex way, the four key elements described in this chapter should be the basis for every written contract. Before writing your own contract or using a sample one, think about what you want it to say. Make sure you are comfortable with all of the terms. If not, change them.

Chapter 5: What Should Be Included in Provider Policies

A contract and provider policies are complimentary tools used to establish and maintain a successful business relationship between parent and provider. The previous chapter described what should be contained in a contract. This chapter will deal with provider policies, the rules and procedures that describe how child care will be given.

Provider policies usually consist of a series of items, and sometimes include a number of forms for parents to fill out. While some providers have many policies and forms, others have very few. It is up to you to decide how much is enough. Keep in mind that certain policies or forms are required in some states. In order for provider policies and forms to serve their purpose, take the time to carefully review them with each parent before the care begins. Some policies may need the input of parents before they can be finalized (particular arrangements for children with special needs, or toilet learning procedures, for example). Some policies may be strictly a matter of what you have decided (for example, the children's activity schedule, you illness policy, and meal and nap time schedules). Forms that you ask parents to complete are often not a matter of negotiation (enrollment forms, medication consent, field trip permission, and so on).

Provider policies cover matters largely controlled by the provider. You can change your policies or add new ones at any time. It is recommended that you state this in your contract and give parents some notice before making changes. Also include in your contract a clause that requires the parent to abide by your policies. For example, "By signing this contract, parent(s)/guardian(s) agree to abide by the written policies of the provider" (see sample contracts in chapter 4).

Some policies will probably be flexible, depending upon the needs of different children. For instance, you might ask, "When would you like Jill to take a nap each day? I prefer between 1:00 and 2:00 in the afternoon, but I am flexible." In other circumstances, you may have an established routine and want to avoid disrupting things. You might say, "Bill, I don't feed breakfast to the other children I care for, and it would be too disruptive if I fed just your child, so I would appreciate it if you fed your child before she comes each morning."

To facilitate the best possible communication with parents and to ensure the most consistent care for children, you should explain each policy and form to parents. Tell them what is negotiable and what is not. If there are some policies that are nonnegotiable, avoid compromising them for one parent as this may cause unhappiness among the other parents. Like the contract, policies and forms should be reviewed at least once a year to see if any changes need to be made. Chapter 6 will discuss how to change contracts and policies in detail.

Let's look at a sample of provider policies and then at a series of forms. Copies of these can be found in the appendix. You can establish whatever policies or forms you want. These samples are only offered as illustrations.

PARENT/PROVIDER POLICIES

Date: _1/1/97_

1. This agreement is made between the Parent(s)/Guardian(s) and Provider for the care of _Danielle and_ _____Joseph Mayer____, (name of child) at the home of the Provider.

2. Substitute Care Arrangements: _Parents will be responsible or Provider will_ _arrange for substitute when she is unavailable._

If the parent/guardian has not notified the provider that he or she will be late, and the provider is unable to continue care, the provider will call one of the authorized persons to come for the child(ren).

3. Persons authorized to pick up the child(ren):

Mother: (Yes)   No   Father: (Yes)   No

Name _John Mayer_   Relationship _Uncle_
Address _21 W 29th St. St Cloud, Mn 56123_
Home phone _731-8942_   Work Phone _749-8123_

Name _Sue Larson_   Relationship _Grandmother_
Address _149 Judson, Oakdale, Mn 55411_
Home phone _491-7177_   Work Phone _____

The provider will allow only persons who have been authorized by the parent/guardian to remove child(ren) from her/his care.

4. Illness Policy:

The parent(s)/guardian(s) agree to notify the provider of a child's illness or suspected illness and to make other arrangements if the child shows any of the following symptoms: _Fever over 101° diarrhea, severe cough, has a_ _contagious illness, or when provider feels child is too ill to be in care_

The provider agrees to attempt to notify the parent/guardian of any illness the child comes in contact with at the provider's home. The provider will attempt to notify the parent(s)/guardian(s) if the child shows any of the following symptoms while in care. The provider may refuse to accept the child for care if these symptoms are present: _Fever, diarrhea, vomiting, or other_ _unusual symptoms_

If, in the opinion of the provider, the child is too ill to remain in care, the parent/guardian will pick up the child when requested by the provider.

5. Emergency Policy:

For life-threatening emergencies, the provider will: _call 911 and parents_

Name of person(s) to call in case of emergency when parent(s) cannot be reached.
Name _John Mayer_   Phone _749-8123_

Name _Sue Larson_   Phone _491-7177_

Page 1 of 2   © 1992 Redleaf Press

---

6. Children with Special Needs

To assure adequate care of _____Danielle_____ , the following is agreed upon:
(name of child)

no wool blankets or feather pillows, only synthetic animals

7. Program Policies: The typical activities for the children are:

Indoor: _Exercise to music puzzles learning activities cutting pasting, painting dress up, blocks singing, fingerplays limited TV, reading_

Outdoor: _Sand box, gymset, riding toys trucks walk to playground nature hikes, sliding & skating in winter, waterplay in summer_

The infant schedule/activities will be: _____

To insure optimal health and welfare of the child(ren), the parent(s)/legal guardian and provider will use the following methods to communicate concerns on the child(ren)'s progress (keep a notebook of daily happenings, talk on the phone once a week, quarterly conferences, etc.): _Notes in cubbie or Spiral notebook with entries of activities, health, milestones, etc. Conference every 3 months_

8. Meals, Naps, Extra Clothing, and Toilet Learning:

The following meals and/or snacks will be provided by the provider: _Breakfast, am snack, lunch, pm snack_

Other food information: _Please don't bring food unless prearranged_

Nap and rest policy will be: _as needed_

The following items of extra clothing will be provided by the parent(s)/legal guardian: _2 extra pair of pants, extra socks, gloves, hat_

_____ Cloth diapers _____ Disposable diapers will be provided by (Parent/Legal Guardian or

Provider):_____

For toilet learning the parent/legal guardian will supply (training pants, extra changes of clothes, etc.):_____

_____

Potty chair will be provided by (Parent/Legal Guardian or Provider): _provider_

Feces will be called _BM or stool_ ; urine will be called _potty or urine_ ;

bowel movements will be called _BM_ ; and urinating will be called _urinating_ .

9. Discipline Policy: Provider rules for disciplining children will be: _Emphasize prevention of problems, no spanking or shaming_

10. Other Issues: Other issues of concern to either parent/legal guardian or provider: _Joseph needs encouragement to talk - extra time on nursery rhymes, singing_

© 1992 Redleaf Press

No portion of this form may be reproduced without permission of the publisher. Contact Redleaf Press, 450 N. Syndicate, Suite 5, St. Paul, Minnesota 55104, 800-423-8309 for information on purchasing additional copies

Notes About Provider Policies
(Numbers correspond to numbered items in the sample provider policies.)

2. Substitute Care Arrangements
Although you may want to keep a list of possible substitutes to care for the children, it is common business practice to make parents responsible for arranging substitute care. Have parents list at least three possible backups. Discuss with the parents the circumstances that must exist before you will call a substitute caregiver from their list (when you are sick, unavailable, or for other emergencies). If you are involved in finding a substitute, make it clear that the parent is hiring the substitute directly, rather than through you. That way you will more likely avoid liability if something goes wrong with the substitute arrangement.

3. Persons Authorized to Pick Up Child in Absence of Parents
To avoid legal trouble, you should have a strict policy of only releasing children to the person(s) who have signed the contract and to those specifically authorized in writing by the parents. The parents should identify at least two other people who are authorized to pick up the child. Ask to keep photos of the authorized persons and, if possible, arrange to meet them so you will recognize them later. If a stranger shows up to claim a child, you should take reasonable steps to stop the person. Do not open your front door to a stranger. Ask the person to leave. Threaten to call the police if the person doesn't leave immediately. You should not try to physically prevent the person from taking the child. If the person takes the child, write down his license plate number and immediately call the police. Next, notify the parent.

Custody Disputes
One morning the mother of one of the children in your care comes to you and says, "My husband and I are in the process of getting a divorce. I'm afraid that he might take our child and flee to another state. I don't want you to allow him to pick up our child anymore." What should you do?

More and more providers find themselves caught in the middle of custody disputes. What is your responsibility? The birth parents of a child are always entitled to custody of the child (including the right to pick up the child from your care at any time), unless a court order limits their rights. You should assume that both parents have full custody rights. A parent has custody rights even if he or she is not listed specifically by the other parent as someone permitted to pick up the child. If one parent presents you with a court order (or divorce decree) that limits the rights of the other parent, you must follow the court order. For instance, if the court order says the father may only have custody of the child on Monday and Wednesday, then you must only allow him to pick up the child on those two days.

How would you respond if the mother asked you not to let the father pick up their child? Your answer might be, "I am sorry, I cannot do what you want. The law says that both parents have a right to pick up the child. I cannot prevent the father from picking up the child unless you show me some type of court order that limits his custody rights. Once you show me such a court order, I will be happy to follow its directions." Make sure the mother understands that it is her responsibility to get a court order and show it to you before you can act. If you are not clear what the court order says, ask the parent for clarification.

❓ *Question: Drunk Driver*

"Occasionally, on Friday afternoons, a parent will come to pick up her child with alcohol on her breath. Sometimes I'm worried whether I should allow her to drive the child home. Can I refuse to give up the child?"

Answer: Know the reporting requirements for the child abuse and neglect laws in your area. If you feel that the child is in imminent danger, child protection laws may require you to report it to the police. Establish a policy to cover this situation. Sit down with each parent and discuss the issue. Here is a suggested policy to follow:

If in the provider's opinion, the parent is not able to transport the child safely, the provider will try to convince the parent not to transport the child. The provider will suggest the following options to the parent:

1) The provider will call a backup who may be able to transport the child in an emergency. The names of the backups are:

Name   Phone #

_____   _____

_____   _____

2) The provider will call a taxi to transport the child. The parent will pay for the taxi.

3) If the parent refuses to agree to one of the above options and insists on leaving with the child, the provider will call the police and report that the driver of the car is intoxicated. *[Note: For this option to be effective, providers need to know the license number of the parents' car. Ask for this when the parents register their child.]*

4) Other options: _____

_____

Make sure the parent understands your intentions. Write out this policy and, because of the sensitive nature of the problem, ask the parent to sign it. If the parent won't sign or doesn't agree with your plan of action, say that you intend to follow it anyway. The safety of the children should be your greatest concern.

Car Seats

Many states have laws that require approved car seats for children. If parents drop off or pick up their children without the proper car seat, you may want to put this requirement in your policies: "Parents must use an approved car seat at all times for drop offs and pick ups." The parent could purchase an extra car seat and leave it with you, to be used when the parent arrives without one. Don't loan the parent a car seat that you own. If there is an accident and the seat is defective, the parent may sue you. Some parents may object to your requirement that they use car seats. They may feel that it is their personal business what they do outside of your home. You should simply tell these parents that the child's safety is your primary concern and that you don't want any unnecessary injuries to occur. If the parents won't agree to your policy, you should seriously consider terminating the business relationship. Most parents will be grateful that your policy shows such concern for the safety of their child.

4. Illness Policy

For the protection of the children and your business, you should exercise caution about caring for children who have a serious contagious illness or are very sick. Recent research indicates that there is less risk than previously thought in caring for children who are recovering from some illnesses. This may mean that you will be more likely to accept children with certain illnesses than you were in the past. You should discuss your illness policy with parents and indicate under what circumstances a doctor will be consulted. If your policy prohibits care for children with certain illnesses, tell parents that you will not accept such children at the morning drop off and that you will expect them to pick up their child immediately if she becomes ill during the day. It is unreasonable for a parent to expect you to care for seriously ill children. In many states, laws prohibit providers from doing so. You should have the final authority about whether or not to care for a sick child. Ask parents to give you updated copies of their child's immunization records to make sure you are protecting the health of all the children in your care. Do not provide care without current immunization records. If a parent refuses to immunize their children regularly, you should seriously consider canceling your contract for the sake of the other children's health.

5. Emergency Policy

You should describe what actions you will take in the event of emergencies such as accidents, poisoning, fire, and poor weather. Keep a copy of emergency numbers near the telephone, as well as the phone numbers of parents and others.

6. Children with Special Needs

State what extra services you will provide for a child with special needs. Your policy should be very flexible and may change for each new child in your care.

? *Question: Behavior Problem*

"One of my children has developed a behavior problem. The parent and I have tried to work out ways to deal with it, but nothing seems to work. The child's behavior is seriously disrupting the other children. What should I do?"

Answer: Seek help from the child's doctor or an outside expert in child development. If the child has a disability that is covered under the Americans with Disabilities Act (ADA), you must make a reasonable effort to do what is necessary to provide care for the child. If the child is not covered by the ADA, you may want to tell the parent to take the child away from your home for a week or so to see if the child will calm down. If nothing works, you may want to terminate your contract with the parent. Perhaps the child will do better with a different provider. Call your local child care resource and referral agency or the Child Care Law Center (see appendix) for help in understanding this law.

7. Program Policies

You may elaborate on the variety of activities and services offered in your business in more or less detail. It is probably not a good idea to include specific times of the day when certain activities will happen. This puts unnecessary pressure on you and may cause the parents to mistrust you if it is not followed exactly.

9. Discipline Policy

Some states regulate discipline policies. If so, you should communicate them to parents. Make sure you do not violate any state rules.

10. Other Issues

Here is an opportunity for parents to offer suggestions about the care of their children. Make sure none of their requests violate any state licensing rules.

Provider Forms

Below is a list of forms that you may or may not want to use with parents. Such forms may be greatly modified to meet your particular needs. Parents should complete these forms before any care is provided. Any changes to the information (such as their address, telephone number, or doctor) should be communicated to you immediately. Once a year you should review all forms with parents and make any necessary changes. Copies of the forms can be found in the appendix.

- Acceptance Form: Use this form to reserve a space for a child and to bind parents to enroll the child on the agreed upon date. Yours could charge a nonrefundable enrollment fee so you would be compensated somewhat if the child does not show up. When the child is enrolled, you could either apply this fee to the first or last weeks of care, or keep the fee as payment for keeping the space open. If the parents objects to paying you for keeping a spot open for their child, you could offer the option of agreeing to care for the child at a future date, but only if a space is open at that time. Offer no guarantee that you will enroll the child. If the parents expect you to guarantee a space in your program sometime in the future, they should expect to pay something for your willingness to turn away other potential clients.

- Medical Form: When the parent is ready to bring the child, use a medical form to collect some basic information about each parent and their children (phone numbers, health history, immunization record, child development, etc.). Have the parent fill out the section dealing with medical emergency consent for treatment. Fill out a new medical form for each child.

- Medication Consent Form: In order to provide medication to the children in your care, you should seek parent authorization. If a doctor is prescribing medicine for a child, get a copy of the doctor's written instructions regarding the administration of the medicine. Require that prescription medication be labeled with the child's name, name of the medication, doctor's name, directions for use, and the expiration date. In addition, you should contact the hospital and doctor you are likely to use in an emergency and ask what special authorization forms they require. Have parents fill out any such forms and return them to the hospital and doctor so they will be on file. At least once a year have parents fill out new permission forms since some hospitals may not accept outdated forms. Find out if state regulations require you to fill out specific medical authorization forms.

- Field Trip Permission Form: It is a good idea to obtain permission from the parents each time you take children on field trips that require a form of transportation such as a car or bus. If this proves to be unmanageable, get parents to sign a general permission form.

- **Receipt for Payment Form:** In order to keep track of parent payments, especially cash payments, give parents a written receipt and keep a copy. You may also use payment receipts as a year-end tax record for both yourself and the parents. Any sales receipt book available in office supply stores may be used.

Provider Philosophy

Some providers give parents a written statement that outlines their personal philosophy of caring for children. Such a philosophy statement could cover the provider's views on child development methods, religious beliefs and how these views will be shared (or not shared) with the children, birthday and special event celebrations, and other details of how the provider runs the business. A philosophy statement can help parents clearly understand what it will be like for their child to receive your care. It can help to stimulate the discussion and clarification of values. Nothing in this philosophy statement should be a matter for parents to negotiate. It is simply a declaration by the provider. The statement could be part of a parent handbook that might also include copies of the contract, provider policies, and any forms.

? Question: Spanking

"A parent wants me to spank her child when she's done something wrong. Our state law allows me to spank the child, but I don't feel comfortable doing it. Should I do what the parent asks?"

Answer: Do not violate your own rules about disciplining children. Tell the parent you won't spank the child because it is against your policy. What goes on in your home is under your control. If the parent doesn't like your policies, tell her you're sorry, but that's the way it is. If local law in your area forbids corporal punishment, you must follow the law, regardless of what you or the parent may want.

In Conclusion

After signing the contract, passing out provider policies, and having parents complete the various forms, everyone will be relieved that the paperwork is over! The next chapter will cover how to make sure that the effort made to come to a child care agreement is not wasted.

Chapter 6:   Making Your Contract and Provider Policies Work

Contracts and provider policies don't solve problems; people do. This chapter will discuss ways to get the most out of contracts and provider policies, specifically:

- How to negotiate terms of a contract and provider policies
- How to change your contract
- How to change your provider policies
- How to enforce your contract and provider policies
- How to terminate your contract

Because many providers are uncomfortable talking about business issues, it may be tempting to just push the papers into the parent's hands and say, "Here's my contract. Please sign it. My policies are attached and you can read them later when you have the time." But a professional provider will resist such urges and will instead take the time with each parent to make sure that they understand what they mean. Verbally explain to the parent some of the key contract provisions. Not all parents will immediately understand all the details of a long written agreement. Ask the parents if they have any questions. One technique is to ask them to explain what a particular contract term or policy means. In asking them to explain part of an agreement in their own words, you may find out that their understanding is different than yours. If necessary, you should change the wording so that everyone clearly agrees with its meaning. Give the parents time to sit down and read the agreement thoroughly. If something isn't clear, make sure you discuss matters until there is mutual understanding. If you are required to have a contract because of local regulations, be sure to let parents know this.

How to Negotiate Terms of a Contract and Provider Policies

As we have discussed in earlier chapters, the terms you put into your contract and provider policies can be just about anything to which you and the parents agree. They don't even have to be the same terms from one parent to another. You should probably assume that parents will find out about the differences, however. Varying provider policies make sense when the needs of a child are unique. These differences can be explained to parents who might ask. If the contract terms are not consistent with each parent, you should have a good reason for doing this. For example, the hours of care stated in your contract may vary from parent to parent. One parent may have been with you for a long time and you give them special privileges, or another parent may be getting a better deal on something because you get something special in return.

Sometimes you will want one term in the contract and a parent wants something else. What do you do? Let's look at one example. Your particular contract may be very different.

Suppose a parent objects to your policy of charging an overtime fee of $3 for every fifteen minutes a child is left in your care beyond the agreed upon hours. How do you resolve this conflict? You have three choices:

1) You can insist on your terms and tell the parent to "take it or leave it."

2) You can try to compromise.

3) You can agree with the parent

Ask for clarification as soon as the parent states an objection. If the parent says something like, "I am insulted by this rule and I won't pay!" you may be justified in assuming that this person will be unreasonable about other issues as well. Avoid signing contracts with parents who don't offer rational arguments to support their objection. If a parent doesn't appreciate your reasons for having overtime fees, you might say, "I'm sorry we don't seem to agree on this, but I am going to have to insist on this overtime fee because I believe it is the best way to run my business."

What if the parent disagrees with you but is more reasonable about it? You may still hold your position or you may want to negotiate a compromise. Find out why this parent has objections and think about a different solution. If you and the parent can't come up with a compromise right away, put off a decision for another day. Ask other providers for their ideas. Let's look at some possible objections parents may have to an overtime fee and some possible compromises. Remember, you can always decide to insist on your terms (and run the risk of losing the parent), or agree with the parent (and not get paid what you believe is fair).

Possible Compromise for Parent Objection
"I can't make the 6:15 P.M. pickup."

- "Can another time be authorized on Wednesdays since you always have late staff meetings on Wednesdays?"

- "What if we renegotiate the fee so you pay more on Wednesday, but less than what the overtime rates would be?"

- "How about if we move the deadline to 6:30 P.M. for you just for Wednesdays?"

"I can't afford to pay such a high overtime fee."

- "What fee do you think is reasonable for my time?"
- "How often do you expect to be late?" (If it's often, don't change your position. If it's not often, suggest a trial period of one month without an overtime fee.)

"I don't have any cash on me when I pick up my child late."

- "Bring your checkbook."
- "Make an advance deposit at the beginning of the month to cover this."
- "I'll let you pay me the next day, but if you don't there will be an additional penalty."

If you agree to compromise, you might try it for a short period of time to see if you're still comfortable with the situation. Let the parent know that it is just a trial period for a specific amount of time and that you will reevaluate it later. It is okay to compromise when you and the parent can talk openly and when both sides agree to give up something during the course of the discussion. Don't compromise over a term in the contract if you feel the parent doesn't respect your position or won't listen to you.

How to Change your Contract

After you've negotiated and signed a contract with a parent, it is good business practice not to make any amendments to it for about a year. There will probably come a day when one party wants to revise the contract. If both you and the parent agree, you can change any term simply by writing a new contract or attaching an amendment to the old one. Any change must be made in writing, however. Let's say you want to raise your rates from $80 to $85 per week. You announce that this will be effective as of January 1, but you don't draw up a new contract. Later in January a parent objects to the higher fee, saying that you never announced it. The parent insists on paying the lower fee until a two week written notice is received. If your contract called for a written notice of any change in the rates, you are stuck. In order to avoid misunderstandings and to protect your legal rights, it is always better to put changes to the contract in writing, have the parent sign them, and make sure the parent has a copy.

If the parent wants to change the contract but you don't, the parent has the choice of giving notice to terminate the contract. You may want to avoid this, but sometimes it may not be possible. Suppose the parent says, "I don't want to have to pay you when my child is ill because I have to pay double when I hire another person to take her when she's sick." Your contract says that parents must pay for up to three sick days a week. If you don't want to change the contract for only one child in your care, you should tell the parent, "I'm sorry, but our contract is clear on this point. If I let you do this all the other parents will want the same.

I can't afford to stay in business if I lose too much income from children who are ill." If the parent does not agree to follow the contract, you should take steps to end the agreement.

If your contract says that parents do not have to pay for any sick days, and you want to change this, follow these steps. Write up the new contract language and present it to all the parents, either in the form of a new contract or an amendment for them to sign. Discuss the details of the change until everyone understands what it means. Give parents some notice before implementing the change, perhaps two to four weeks.

The best way to make sure that any changes in your contract are handled smoothly is to conduct a regular review of its terms with the parents. Sit down and go over the contract in detail with each parent, ideally every six months, but at least once a year. Such a semiannual review fosters communication and reminds both parties of their responsibilities. Make sure the contract says what you think it does and correct anything that is out of date.

How to Change Your Provider Policies

Not having a written policy is better than having a written policy and not following it. Use the semiannual review to make sure you're following your own rules. For example, if you're not taking a field trip every week as the policy states, parents who later violate your policies may argue that you aren't living up to the policies either. Although such an attempt by the parent to shift blame will probably not be justified, you can avoid this problem by regularly reviewing your policies to make sure you are following your own rules. As mentioned in chapter 5, you can change your provider policies at will, with or without any notice to parents. It is more professional, however, to give parents some notice before making any changes.

How to Enforce Your Contract and Provider Policies

For many providers, trying to enforce their contract and provider policies is one of the most difficult aspects of their job. When feelings of anger and frustration with parents begin to grow, many providers would prefer not to deal with conflict at all and hope it will go away. Some don't speak up to a parent because they are afraid that they might be wrong or that the parent will get angry or terminate the agreement.

A contract and provider policies don't mean much unless both parties take them seriously and expect each other to live up to the terms. This is true even when relatives or close friends sign agreements. You have made a business contract that can be enforced against you, so you should be prepared to enforce it. A contract won't protect you unless you follow its terms and insist that the parents do likewise. For example, what if your contract calls for payments to be made for days when a child is sick? If you don't actually enforce this rule for six months and then take the parent to court for not paying for sick days, you may not win. By not following the contract term earlier, you led the parent to believe that it was not going to be enforced. Although provider policies may not be enforceable in court, you should make an equal effort to see that you and the parent follow the rules. If some policies are ignored by either party, it tends to undermine the trust in a relationship.

Certainly it is easier to enforce a written contract or provider policies than verbal ones. You can pull out an agreement, point out a term to the parent and say, "This is what you agreed to do." Yet many providers can't get up enough nerve to do this. If you don't feel confident enough to take the initiative to confront a parent, try these suggestions:

1) Set up frequent meetings with parents, perhaps monthly, to review how things are going. Sometimes it is easier to bring up a problem at a regularly scheduled meeting.

2) Write a note to the parent pointing out the problem. "Yesterday, January 12, your child was dropped off without a hat or mittens and she couldn't play outside. Please remember to bring them tomorrow." Give the note to the parent directly; don't slip it in the diaper bag or hand it to the child.

3) Talk about the problem to another provider, licensing/regulation worker, or friend. Ask for support in how to deal with the parent.

4) Ask the local resource and referral service or another provider to mediate between you and the parent.

For minor deviations from the contract or provider policies, it is a good idea to use the written agreement as a tool for communication. Take it out and show it to the parent when a rule has been broken. Get into the habit of bringing up all violations of the contract or provider policies so the parent will know that the rules are not haphazardly enforced. If you are breaking a rule, tell the parent what you are doing to correct your behavior. A simple apology may be all that is needed from you or the parent to keep things working well.

The contract and provider policies should be seen as a guide to behavior. Don't feel like you are an ogre for bringing up a violation. When a problem does arise, try talking it out. Set aside a time and place to talk when neither of you will be disturbed. Before you meet, think through what you want to say and write out the main points. To keep things from becoming personal, stick to the issue at hand and try to relate the problem to a specific term in the written agreement. When talking to the parent, try to control your emotions and express your concern. Keep the children out of any dispute. Focus on behaviors, not attitudes. You may feel that a parent has a bad attitude about life, but what you really want changed is the fact that this parent always pays you on Wednesday instead of Monday. Listen to the problems of the parent, but be clear about what you want done. You may be able to satisfactorily resolve minor violations in an informal manner.

If the violations are serious or repeated, it may be time to enforce the rules: "Ellery, this is the second time you've picked up your child late this month. Our contract calls for you to pay an overtime fee when this happens. I've not asked for payment until now because I've tried to be understanding of your schedule. But you've violated our agreement too often and so, as of next Wednesday, I will have to start enforcing our contract. Do you understand?"

The Basic Rules of Enforcement

There must be consequences for not following the rules you have included in your contract and policies. Without consequences, your agreement will be difficult to enforce. It is not enough to simply state that "Parents must give a two-week notice before removing their child from care." What happens if the parent leaves without giving a two-week notice? What will be the consequence to the parent? Since the contract doesn't say that the parent must pay for this time, it will be difficult for the judge to award damages. Instead, the provider should add to the above statement, "Payment by the parent is due for the notice period, whether or not the child is brought to the provider for care." Now the provider has clearly stated the consequence for not giving a two week-notice.

Providers can choose among a wide variety of consequences for their contract and policy terms. The ultimate consequence for a violation of any part of the agreement is termination. But look at what other consequences are possible:

Example: Parent fails to pick up child on time
A parent regularly fails to pick up her child at the proper time (5:30 P.M.). Here are some possible consequences to add to the contract:

1) Parent must pay $1 per minute for every minute after 5:30 P.M. that the parent is late in picking up the child. Payment is due the same day.

2) If the parent notifies the provider by 5:45 P.M. that she will be late, no late fee will be imposed. Otherwise, the parent will pay a flat late fee of $10.

3) If a parent fails to pick up the child by 6:00 P.M., the provider may choose to have another caregiver take the child for care. The client must pay the caregiver for the time she provides care. *[Note: For this option, have the parents sign an agreement ahead of time that allows you to bring their child to another caregiver.]*

4) The parent will give the names of two people who can pick up the child in an emergency. If the parent has not notified the provider by 5:45 P.M. of when the client will be picking up the child, the provider may decide to have the child picked up by one of the backup names.

5) Parents who fail to pick up their child by 5:30 P.M. will be given a warning. Failure to pick up a child on time after a second warning will result in immediate termination of the contract.

6) Parents who fail to pick up their child by 5:30 P.M. will have their contract terminated immediately.

Some of these consequences could also be used if a parent refuses to pay on time or if a parent refuses to immediately pick up their child when the child becomes sick during the day.

There are many other examples of consequences a provider could adopt. All of the ones cited above are perfectly legal. You don't have to adopt any of these consequences.

Two Key Contract Terms

Although providers have the freedom to set their own contract terms, here are two that are strongly recommend to every provider:

1) Parents must pay in advance for the child care services.

2) Parents must pay a two-week deposit, in advance, which will be applied to the last two weeks of care.

These rules give the provider financial security. If a parent walked out today, the provider would still be paid for the rest of that week, plus two more weeks. The provider can use this time to find another client without a loss of income. These rules also give the provider power. Often providers are reluctant to enforce their rules because they are fearful the parent will leave owing them money. With this fear gone, providers may be more assertive about enforcing rules and will probably have fewer conflicts with parents. Providers generally have very few problems with parents when they set clear rules and consequences for not following them. Providers who have the most trouble with parents are those who don't have clear rules and are inconsistent in enforcing them.

If you would like to add these two key terms to the contract you are presently using, simply prepare a new contract with the new terms included. Notify parents of the change at least one month in advance. Let's say you give the new contract to the parent on January 1, with the new terms to go into effect on March 1 (which is a Monday). If you charge $90 a week, you announce to the parent that you expect to be paid $90 on March 1 for that week, and another $180 as a deposit for the last two weeks of care, whenever they may be. Later, when the parent decides to leave, the last two weeks are already paid. If the client leaves without giving the proper two-week notice, you keep the $180.

There are several strategies you can suggest to negotiate the period of transition. Here are two options for having the parent pay in advance each week:

1) The parent continues to pay on Friday, but pays an extra $5 or $10 each week until $90 is accumulated by the provider. Then the parent goes back to paying $90 each Friday. With the extra $90 paid in advance, the parent is now really paying for the following week when she pays the provider on Friday.

2) The provider allows the parent more time to transition into the new schedule. The parent pays $5 or $10 on Monday, March 1 and the remaining weekly amount on that Friday. The next Monday (March 8) the parent pays $10 or $15 and the balance on Friday. This continues until the full $90 is being paid on Monday.

Both of these options are financially affordable to nearly every parent when given enough advance notice and a low payment of $5 or $10 a week. It is up to the provider to negotiate a reasonable payment plan and stick to it. This means that providers should enforce their own late payment consequences on any parent who does not meet the agreed upon payment schedule.

To get the parent to pay the $180 two-week deposit in advance, ask the parent to make an extra payment each week of $10 or $15 until the full amount is reached. Nearly every parent can afford paying a little more each week for a limited time if given enough advance notice. Again, the provider should enforce a penalty if the parent doesn't make payments when they are due.

If you charge by the hour, you could ask the parent to pay a deposit on Monday of an amount equal to what the parent normally pays in a week. At the end of the week you could refund any unused amount or carry it over into the next week. If the parent deposit was not enough, the extra can be added to the next week's deposit. Even though this method calls for you to do more record keeping, it keeps you in control of the finances.

Requiring parents to pay in advance and pay a two-week deposit are reasonable business rules. However, they may be harder to introduce in a community where few other providers have these rules. Providers should know what is common practice in their community before changing their rules. Providers who offer quality care and are flexible about implementing these new rules over time usually do not have trouble making such changes.

Even though you care about the child very much, sometimes the frustration and hassle with the parents is just not worth it. When you are trying to enforce the contract or provider policies, you should always be prepared to tell the parent to leave if you aren't able to work things out. If parents know you are serious about enforcing the rules, they will be less likely to try to take advantage of you.

Raising Your Rates

Many providers are surprised to learn that providers just starting out often charge higher rates than providers who have been in business for many years. This is because providers tend not to raise their rates on a regular basis after starting their business. Providers are often shy about raising their rates and are uncomfortable talking with parents about this. Some providers feel intimidated when parents question them about their rates. Providers should consider raising their rates on a regular basis, even if the raise is very small.

Providers are not obligated to give parents any reason for their annual rate increases. If providers feel the need to explain themselves, here are some reasons that could be given for a rate increase:

1) "My expenses (food, toys, utilities, insurance, etc.) have gone up this year."

2) "I have one more year of experience as a provider that enables me to offer higher quality care for your child."

3) "I have some special business expenses this year (swing set, computer, etc.) that need to be paid."

Not surprisingly, parents are not always supportive of rate increases. This should not deter providers. Parents usually receive raises on a regular basis at their place of work and should expect to pay more for child care over time. Providers should put a term in the contract that states when rate increases will happen. One way to avoid this is to activate rate increases on the anniversary date of when the child was first enrolled. If the parent refuses to pay the higher rate, the provider should let the parent know that the termination clause in their contract will be enforced.

Instead of raising rates, providers may want to consider charging additional fees to increase their income. Such additional fees may be for registration, liability insurance, field trips, activity supplies, sick days, or vacations.

Providers may also want to raise the rates they charge for infant care. Because the demand for infant care is greater, parents will pay more. Providers probably will have an easier time raising rates for infants than any other age group. To find out more about rates and fee policies in your community, contact your local child care resource and referral agency.

Using the Minimum Wage as a Guideline for Setting Your Rates

One way to look at setting your rates is to compare your hourly net income to the federal minimum wage of $4.75 per hour ($5.15 per hour as of October 1, 1997). Let's look at an example:

Provider's Current Income

Parent A: toddler	$95/week X 50 weeks =	$4,750
Parent B: preschooler	$80/week X 50 weeks =	$4,000
Parent C: preschooler	$80/week X 30 weeks =	$2,400
Parent D: preschooler	$80/week X 40 weeks =	$3,200
Parent E: school-ager	$50/week X 50 weeks =	$2,500
Parent F: school-ager	$50/week X 50 weeks =	$2,500
Parent G: school-ager	$50/week X 50 weeks =	$2,500
Adult and Child Care Food Program Income		$3,000
Total Income:		$24,850

Current Expenses

Food	$3,500
House expenses	$3,200
Car expenses	$ 300
Supplies/Toys	$2,000
Household items	$1,300
Depreciation	$1,000
Taxes	$2,800
Total Expenses:	$14,100
Net income (profit):	*$10,750*

Hours worked:	55 hours per week X 50 weeks = 2,750 hours
Hourly wage:	$10,750 ÷ 2,750 hours = $3.91 per hour
	$13,063 ÷ 2,750 hours = $4.75 per hour

In this example the provider is earning $3.91 per hour, based on $10,750 of profit and 2,750 hours of work. To earn the minimum wage of $4.75 per hour, this provider must earn an additional $2,313 per year (2,750 hours multiplied by $4.75), or $46.26 per week ($2,313 divided by 50 weeks). If this amount was divided equally among the seven children, it amounts to a raise of $6.60 per week. This is a 10.6% overall increase in rates. Providers are encouraged to take a look at how many hours they work at their business and compare

Safe Havens — by Bill Holbrook

© 1991, Washington Post Writers Group. Reprinted with permission.

this to their profit (don't forget to including the hours you spend on such duties as record keeping, cleaning, and activity preparation). Most providers earn less than the minimum wage. Although it may not be possible to immediately raise your rates in order to reach the minimum wage, you may want to use this as a goal to meet within the next few years.

Price Fixing

In all of the following situations, there is probably a violation of the federal antitrust law:

- At an association meeting, family child care providers discuss how much they charge parents.

- In order to find out the going rate in her neighborhood, a new provider calls another provider and asks what she charges parents.

- A family child care association surveys its members about rates and shares the results at the next association meeting.

Federal antitrust laws are designed to encourage competition and discourage competitors from setting prices higher than they would be otherwise. When providers discuss rates at association meetings it can easily be construed to be a discussion to raise rates. This is true even if there are no direct statements made encouraging providers to raise rates. Associations that operate their own referral service for parents can give rate information to parents who call the service, but they cannot share this information with other providers in the association.

Rate information can be shared legally when:

1) An individual or organization other than an association collects the rate information and makes it readily available to the public, not just to one association.

2) The information is communicated in such a way that doesn't allow a person to identify the rates of a specific provider.

3) The sample of providers surveyed is large enough so that no one can identify the rates of any one provider.

Providers or associations can share rate information collected by resource and referral agencies or by county agencies who use it to determine the subsidy rate for low-income parents. If a provider or association wants to know the rates for a small geographic area, for accredited providers, or for new providers, they should have an independent organization do the survey (perhaps the resource and referral agency) and make sure the results are widely distributed to the public.

Many providers and associations have unknowingly violated the federal antitrust law. Recently, the Minnesota Attorney General's office investigated one provider association and ordered it to stop sharing rate information at their meetings. After promising not to do this in the future, the state took no further action against the association. It is very unlikely that a state will ever fine a provider or an association who is unknowingly breaking the law.

How to Terminate Your Contract

When the Parent Ends the Contract
You should understand that in a majority of situations it is the parent who will decide to end the relationship, even when you are doing a good job. Parents usually leave a provider because they are changing jobs, moving to another town, or simply because their child is growing older. If the parent is leaving due to dissatisfaction, hopefully you won't be surprised when you receive a notice. Previous discussions and attempts at compromise will probably let you know there is a serious problem that hasn't been resolved. It may be useful to discuss the problem once more to see if a solution can be found. If not, pull out the contract and remind the parent, if it is necessary, about the agreed upon termination period.

When the Provider Ends the Contract
You may have many reasons for wanting to end an agreement with a parent: the parent constantly breaks the rules, you want to care for fewer children, a child is too difficult to manage, etc. But you don't need to have any particular reason to end the contract. You can always say, "I've decided not to care for your child anymore, Kathy. Your last day will be two weeks from tomorrow."

Of course it is always better to try working out any problems with a parent before you decide to terminate the contract. Discuss problems with the parent as they arise rather than putting them off. When a conflict arises, make it a practice to take notes about what happened (see chapter 2 for an example). You can use these notes to help you clarify the problem and communicate better with a parent. Talk to your licensing worker about what you might be able to do differently to resolve things. Seek other outside help if you can. Maybe a friend, nurse, or social worker might have good suggestions. Don't assume that there is only one answer to a problem or that your solution is always the best one. If you can show flexibility about solving problems, you will reduce your stress and the stress of the child and parent.

Don't be afraid to negotiate a solution with the parent: "How about if we try your suggestion this week and then my idea next week?" or "I'll not charge you for your child's absence this week, but I'd like you to pick up your child a half hour early next Friday so I can make a doctor's appointment. Agreed?" Remember, you can set aside your own rules and negotiate a new solution with any parent.

When should you terminate your contract with a parent? Most providers don't terminate their contract without good reason. Some good reasons include: the parent is violating your contract or policies, the child's behavior is disruptive beyond your control, or your general anxiety or stress level is higher than you want it to be. In other words, you just may be too hassled to cope anymore with either the parent or the child. There is nothing wrong with terminating a contract simply to give yourself a much needed break from the stress.

If you are seriously considering ending the contract, follow these steps:

1) Refer to your contract or policies to point out the problem to the parent: "You did not give me four-weeks notice of your vacation, Francis, as required under the terms of our contract. If it happens again, I'll have to give you your notice."

2) Give a written warning that states the contract will be terminated unless the parent's behavior changes.

3) Be specific about what the parent needs to do to avoid future conflicts: "Give me proper notice of your vacations," "Pick up your child within forty-five minutes when she becomes ill."

Don't let it be a surprise to the parent when you finally give notice to terminate the contract. Make it clear ahead of time that unless something changes, you will give notice. When you do decide to end the relationship, make sure you carefully follow the termination procedure in your contract. Give the length of notice promised in the contract and put your notice in writing.

Sample Termination Notice

This note is to let you know that I will not be able to offer my child care services to
_____ (child's name) beginning on, _____ (date).
I will continue to provide my regular child care services until this date. According to
our written contract, you are required to pay for my services up until this date, whether
or not your child is present.

_____   _____
Provider Signature   Date

_____   _____
Parent Signature   Date

Keep your termination notice short and simple. You do not want to give explanations for why your are terminating the contract. The parent should already understand the problem and be aware that you are unhappy with the situation. If you've reached the stage of giving out a termination notice, restating the problem would only further aggravate the parent. You simply want to announce that the contract will be terminated and explain how details of the last days of care will be handled.

Maintain a professional attitude in the way you treat both the parent and the child during the notice period. You might offer to give the parent the number of the local child care resource and referral agency where the parent can look for another provider. If you follow the above procedures, you will get through the termination process without any unnecessary bad feelings.

Chapter 7:   Enforcing Your Contract in Court

A contract is a legal document that can be enforced in a court of law. The vast majority of contract disputes between providers and parents, however, never end up in court. When a parent violates one of your policies, you can end the contract. When a parent owes you money, you can take them to court. Before doing that, however, you should use several strategies for resolving the matter. This chapter will discuss how to resolve problems before going to court and, when necessary, how to prepare for court.

Most problems between providers and parents are caused by misunderstandings and a lack of clear communication on both sides. Take time to talk with parents about problems or concerns as they arise. If a problem becomes major, you should consider using mediation before suing parents in small-claims court.

Mediation

Mediation is a voluntary process to help parties with a disagreement reach their own solution. Some areas of the country have mediation centers which will provide a neutral mediator to help resolve the problem. The cost to use this type of service is usually very small. Ask your local legal aid society or bar association if there is a mediation center in your area. If not, you may want to seek out a neutral person (a pastor, rabbi, or counselor, for example) who might be willing to serve as a mediator for your situation.

There are a number of advantages to using a mediator to try resolving your problem:

1) A mediator may be able to solve the controversy more quickly than going to court.

2) Using a mediator is less intimidating to most providers than going to court.

3) The mediation process is confidential, unlike a court hearing.

4) Mediation can create a situation where both parties win, encouraging a creative, flexible solution and avoiding the adversarial win/lose atmosphere that characterizes most courtrooms.

5) When both parties contribute to a solution, they are more likely to follow through with it. Even if you win in small-claims court, you may have trouble collecting your money.

6) You still have the option of going to small-claims court.

7) If the parent is unwilling to use a mediation process, you can tell this to the judge. Doing so increases your credibility.

The "Demand" Letter

If the parent owes you money, it is up to you to decide whether or not to go to court over it. Before starting a lawsuit, ask the parent for payment. Try to find a solution: "I'm willing to accept payment of $20 a week for the next six weeks, James." If the parent refuses to live up to his agreement or doesn't meet a payment schedule, write the parent a "demand" letter. Send the letter by registered mail so you can prove that it was received. Make sure you keep a copy for your own files. The "demand" letter should contain these elements:

1) The dates you cared for the child

2) The amount of money the parent owes you and why

3) A demand for payment by a specific date

4) A notice that you intend to take legal action if the parent does not respond to the letter by a specific date

5) Your signature and the date you signed the letter.

The "demand" letter informs the parent that you are serious about collecting the money you are owed. You can still decide not to sue the parent even after making threats to do so in your "demand" letter, however the threat of a lawsuit may convince the parent to pay, as most people do not want to be taken to court.

If the parent refuses to pay after receiving your letter, you must decide whether or not to go to court. You may decide to drop the matter if the parent doesn't have any money, the amount owed is very small, or you don't want to take the time to appear in court. If you do sue, get ready for court by collecting all the necessary records, such as a copy of your contract, your "demand" letter, and any other written notes. Write a memo to yourself that describes the events leading up to your decision to sue so you won't forget the details.

Sample "Demand" Letter

August 1, 1997
Lucy Stone
1453 Collier Ave
Garden City, Kansas 17689

Dear Lucy;

I provided child care services for your daughter, Mary, from January 1, 1997 to June 28, 1997 at a fee of $82 per week. On June 28, 1997 you informed me you would not be bringing Mary back any more. At that time you owed me $82 for the week of June 24-28.

You did not give me a two week written notice, which our contract requires. You owe me $164 for this two week notice period (July 1 to July 12, 1997).

I am requesting that you pay me $246 by August 15, 1997. If I do not hear from you by then, I will have no choice but to take legal action against you, at which time I will sue you for $164, plus late charges and all court costs.

Paula Provider

Paula Provider

Going to Small-Claims Court

Most states have small-claims court (sometimes called conciliation court) where people can bring lawsuits for small amounts of money, usually between $7,500 to $10,000. Check with your local county courthouse to find out how you file a lawsuit. Small-claims court is designed to be an informal and inexpensive way to settle disputes. In most states, lawyers are not encouraged to represent the parties. The process to file a lawsuit usually follows this pattern:

- You file your lawsuit by completing a simple form in which you state that the parent violated your contract. You will probably have to file your lawsuit in the county in which the parent lives and you will need to know the parent's current address.

- You may have to pay a small fee to file your lawsuit. Add this fee to the amount you are suing the parent.

- The court will probably notify you and the parent by mail of the date and time of your court hearing. The waiting time between the filing date and the hearing can be a few weeks or several months.

- After getting the notice of the court hearing, the parent may countersue you, claiming that you violated the contract.

At the Hearing

Arrive at the courtroom at least twenty minutes before the time of your hearing. Look around the room and try to relax. If the parent doesn't show up for the hearing, the judge is likely to enter a judgment in your favor. Before the case begins, the judge may ask you to try reaching a settlement. Consider taking this chance to work things out. If you can't, you will be called before the judge, sworn in, and asked to tell your side of the story.

Tips for making your best case in court

- Be well-prepared. Bring a chronology of conversations, phone calls, letters, and other events surrounding the dispute.

- Use notes to help you remember important points. You may have only one chance to tell your story.

- Bring evidence. For example, copies of the signed contract, copies of your letter to the parent, or copies of returned checks. Offer these to the judge.

- Stay focused and stick to the facts. Your case is weakened if you ramble or aren't sure of your facts.

- If you want to use the testimony of a witness, the witness must appear with you in court. Most courts will not allow written affidavits.

- Inform the judge if the parent refused your offer to try mediation.

- If the parent raises child abuse allegations in court as an excuse for not paying you, deny the allegations quickly and get back to the real issue.

- If the parent raises an issue you've never heard, point that out. You can say, "You never told me that before," or "You never complained to my licensor about that."

- Stay calm. You weaken your case by entering a shouting match with the parent. If the parent makes statements to which you object, ask the judge if you may respond to those statements and do so calmly.

The main thing to remember when planning for a court appearance is that you will have a very short time to speak. You must stay focused on the fact that the parent violated the contract. Here's an example of what a provider might want to say:

"Your honor, I am Barbara Neilson. I provided child care for Mrs. Taylor for six months. Last November 1 she left without giving me a two-week notice, in violation of our contract. Here is a copy of our contract which requires her to give me a two-week notice when she wishes to leave. I asked her to pay. I wrote a letter requesting that she pay. She has refused. I am asking the court to enforce our contract. Thank you."

Sometimes a parent will raise side issues in court and attempt to argue that she shouldn't have to give the two-week notice. The parent may say, "I was unhappy because the provider wouldn't follow my instructions and make sure my child did not take a nap in the afternoon. This makes it very difficult for me to get my child to go to bed at night." The way to respond to such parent complaints is not to argue about it. It usually doesn't matter if the parent's story is true or not. What is important is that the parent broke the contract. Your response might be, "Your honor, I had discussions with the parent about when her child should take naps. If the parent was unhappy with my policy, she has a right to take her child away. But she must do so according to our agreement. She did not do so. A parent should not be able to get away with breaking the contract every time she is unhappy."

The only circumstances under which a parent might legitimately get out of a contract is if her child's health or safety are in immediate danger. For instance, if the provider is allowing the children to play in the street, or the children are being physically or emotionally abused. These situations are very rare. The provider can argue that the parent never made the complaint to the proper authorities, usually the licensing worker. If the parent did complain to licensing and it was determined that the complaint was not credible, the provider should point this out to the judge.

How Well Do Providers Fare in Court?

There is no guarantee that you will win your case in court, no matter how carefully you've prepared your contract. You are very likely to be awarded the money for the days you provided care for a child in which the parent did not pay. It is more difficult to win for a non-payment of a two-week notice period. Providers who have a contract term that specifically calls for parents to pay during the two-week notice period, whether or not the child is present, are more likely to win court decisions than providers who have a contract that simply states, "Parents must give a two-week notice" (see contract #2 in the appendix). Judges do not always enforce a two-week notice period in contracts between providers and parents. They should. Unless there are some unusual circumstances (such as health and safety issues), the contract is binding. Unfortunately, some judges do not treat the provider/parent relationship with enough respect. Even so, providers should pursue their case in court.

How to Collect Payment from Parents if You Win in Small-Claims Court

Most small-claims courts will notify both parties by mail of the judge's decision within a few weeks of the court hearing. If you win, the parent is notified that they must pay you within a definite time period (usually no more than thirty days). If they don't pay by then, it is up to you to pursue the parent for payment. Ask the office clerk at the small-claims court about the procedures for collection. You may have to pay a small fee to have the sheriff's office collect the debt. You are responsible for giving the sheriff's office enough information to collect it. This includes the name of the parents' bank and their bank account number, or the parents' place of employment. Ask for this information when the parents first register their child. The sheriff's office can then seize the money from the parent's paycheck or bank account. They may even be able to put a lien on the parent's house so that it cannot be sold until the parents pay you. Although it may take some time to collect, you will probably get the money.

If You Lose Your Case in Small-Claims Court

In most states you have the option of appealing the court's decision if you lose in small-claims court. Usually this must be done within a short period of time from when you receive the notice from the court. Ask the clerk at the small-claims court for the procedures you must follow to appeal. Appeals are often handled by attorneys and require significantly higher filing fees than small-claims cases.

If you do lose your case, try not to be too discouraged. Here are some coping strategies that may help:

- Recognize that the justice system is not perfect and that some things happen to us that are not fair.

- Think of the experience as an opportunity to learn how the court works so that you will be better prepared next time.

- Rework your contract to avoid the same problem. Talk with the other parents to clarify what you both agreed to.

- Write a letter to the parent. List everything you dislike about them as savagely as you want. Put it away in a drawer and don't send it.

- Maintain your sense of humor. Life is too short to worry about an amount of money that won't let you retire any earlier.

Safe Havens   by Bill Holbrook

© 1991, Washington Post Writers Group. Reprinted with permission.

How to Hire a Lawyer

There may come a time in the course of your business when you need a lawyer to defend yourself against a lawsuit by a parent or to help you sue someone. Like many people, most providers have little contact with lawyers. Finding one to represent you can be a challenge. If you are sued, first check your insurance policies to see if you are entitled to receive legal assistance. Ask around for the names of attorneys who have handled legal cases similar to yours. Talk to your tax preparer, insurance agent, friends, local child care resource and referral agency, local bar association, and other providers.

When you have identified some attorneys, shop around as you would for any other service. Ask each attorney you have identified for fifteen minutes to discuss your problem. Many attorneys will not charge you for your first consultation. Meet with at least three, if you can. Ask for references and call them to find out how satisfied they were with the attorney's work. When deciding whether or not to hire an attorney, consider these criteria:

1) Fees: Ask up front what the attorney would charge for a case like yours. Some charge by the hour, some work for a fixed fee.

2) Compatibility: Pick an attorney you feel comfortable with and can talk with easily.

3) Experience: Has the attorney handled other cases like yours?

4) Location: Is the attorney's office convenient to your home?

5) Size of law firm: Smaller firms may tend to charge less than large firms.

When you meet with an attorney, bring all your documents and try to be as clear as you can about your problem. Once you have chosen an attorney, have your agreement put in writing; you're making another contract.

For further information, see the Child Care Law Center publication *How to Find and Use a Lawyer* (listed in the appendix).

A Final Word

This book explains how written agreements and policies can be used to communicate more effectively with parents. Using these tools can give you more time to concentrate on your job of caring for children. The key to dealing with parents is setting limits and sticking to your agreement. You are running a business and must make decisions that will enable you to provide high quality care and stay in business.

It may not be easy to adopt all of the recommendations in this book at once. You should move at a comfortable pace. You may want to start by using short written agreements. As you gain more experience, more detailed contracts and provider policies may follow.

It has been the intention in this book to empower providers to become more successful in managing their business dealings with parents. It is my hope that doing so will contribute to attracting and retaining more professional providers to this field. In the end this will result in the best possible care for children.

If you have questions regarding contracts and policies, or if you have suggestions on how this book could be improved, address them to Tom Copeland at Redleaf National Institute, 450 North Syndicate Avenue, Suite 5, St. Paul, MN 55104. My e-mail address is fzpg63a@Prodigy.com.

APPENDIX

Sample Contracts, Provider Policies, and Other Forms

I. Sample #1: Basic Contract

1. This contract is made between the Parent(s)/Guardian(s) and Provider for the care of _____, (name of child) at the home of the Provider.

2. The payment fee shall be: $_____ per week / hour
   Payment shall be due on _____.

3. This contract may be terminated by either Parent(s)/Guardian(s) or Provider by giving a _____-week written notice in advance of the ending date. The Provider may immediately terminate the contract without giving any notice if the Parent(s)/Guardian(s) do not make payments when due.

4. The signature of the Parent(s)/Guardian(s) to this contract also indicates that they agree to abide by the written policies of the Provider. The Provider may change these written policies from time to time.

_____   _____
Mother/Guardian   Father/Guardian

_____   _____
Home Address   Home phone

_____   _____
Business Phone   Business Phone

_____   _____
Provider   Date Contract Signed

Sample #2: Provider-Parent/Guardian Child Care Agreement

The following agreement is made between:

1. _____   _____   _____
     Mother/Legal Guardian   Home Phone   Work Phone

     _____
     Home Address

     _____
     Employer's Name and Address

and

2. _____   _____   _____
     Father/Legal Guardian   Home Phone   Work Phone

     _____
     Home Address

     _____
     Employer's Name and Address

and

3. _____
     Child Care Provider   Phone

     _____
     Address

for the care of:

4. _____   _____ ;
     Child's Name/Date of Birth   Child's Name/Date of Birth

     _____   _____
     Child's Name/Date of Birth   Child's Name/Date of Birth

Basic Rates and Payment Policies:

The payment fee shall be $_____ per week or $_____ per day or $_____ per hour.

Care shall be provided normally from _____ a.m. to _____ p.m. on these days: (Circle all that apply)

Monday   Tuesday   Wednesday   Thursday   Friday   Saturday   Sunday.

Additional Fees: _____

_____

Payment shall be due on: _____.

Overtime Rates:

1. For the purpose of this agreement, overtime will be considered as drop-off before _____ a.m. _____ p.m.

   and pick-up after _____ a.m. _____ p.m.

2. If the parent/legal guardian makes prior arrangements with the provider, the child may stay overtime at the

   following rate: $_____ per _____ or portion thereof.

3. If the parent/legal guardian has not informed the provider that he or she will be arriving earlier or later than the

   agreed upon times, the following rate will be charged: $_____ per _____ or portion thereof.

         © 1991 Redleaf Press

A preprinted version of this form is available from Redleaf Press, 800-423-8309.

Rates Regarding Holidays, Vacations and Other Absences:

1. The following are paid holidays when they fall on a day regularly scheduled for care: _____
_____

2. Charges for a child's absence will be:_____
_____

3. Charges related to provider's illness or other emergency that prohibit care will be: _____
_____

4. Charges related to provider's scheduled vacation are: _____
_____

5. Charges related to parent(s)/guardian's scheduled vacation are: _____
_____

The provider and the parent/guardian will each give _____ weeks advance notice of scheduled vacation or other leave.

6. Other: _____

Other Charges:

1. There will be a charge of $_____ for each breakfast, $_____ for each lunch, and $_____ for each snack served. Other: _____

2. There will be an extra charge for the following infant supplies when not provided by the parent(s)/legal guardian:
_____

    diapers, wipes, baby food, formula, etc.

and for activity fees/expenses for _____

    field trips, children's classes, materials for special projects, etc.

3. A holding fee (deposit) of _____ is required to be paid on _____ which will be applied to the _____ week's payment or forfeited if the child does not come for care as agreed.

Termination Procedure:

This contract may be terminated by either parent/guardian or provider by giving _____ weeks written notice in advance of the ending date. Payment by parent/guardian is due for the notice period, whether or not the child is brought to the provider for care. The provider may terminate the contract without giving any notice if the parent/guardian does not make payments when due. Failure by the provider to enforce one or more terms of the contract does not waive the right of the provider to enforce any other terms of the contract.

Signatures:

By signing this contract, parent(s)/guardian(s) agree to abide by the written policies of the provider. The provider may amend the policies by giving the parent(s)/guardian(s) a copy of the new or changed policies at least _____ weeks before they go into effect.

Provider's signature _____ Date _____

Mother/Legal Guardian's signature _____ Date _____

Father/Legal Guardian's signature _____ Date _____

Co-signer's signature _____ Date _____

If the parent or legal guardian is under age 18, a co-signer must sign this agreement and act as a guarantor to the contract and agree to be bound by all financial terms.

Page 2 of 2

© 1991 Redleaf Press

II. Parent/Provider Policies

Date:_____

1. This agreement is made between the Parent(s)/Guardian(s) and Provider for the care of_____

_____, (name of child) at the home of the Provider.

2. Substitute Care Arrangements:_____

_____

If the parent/guardian has not notified the provider that he or she will be late, and the provider is unable to continue care, the provider will call one of the authorized persons to come for the child(ren).

3. Persons authorized to pick up the child(ren):

| Mother: | Yes | No | Father: | Yes | No |

Name_____ Relationship _____

Address_____

Home phone _____ Work Phone _____

Name _____ Relationship _____

Address _____

Home phone _____ Work Phone _____

The provider will allow only persons who have been authorized by the parent/guardian to remove child(ren) from her/his care.

4. Illness Policy:

The parent(s)/guardian(s) agree to notify the provider of a child's illness or suspected illness and to make other arrangements if the child shows any of the following symptoms:_____

_____

The provider agrees to attempt to notify the parent/guardian of any illness the child comes in contact with at the provider's home. The provider will attempt to notify the parent(s)/guardian(s) if the child shows any of the following symptoms while in care. The provider may refuse to accept the child for care if these symptoms are present: _____

_____

If, in the opinion of the provider, the child is too ill to remain in care, the parent/guardian will pick up the child when requested by the provider.

5. Emergency Policy:

For life-threatening emergencies, the provider will: _____

_____

Name of person(s) to call in case of emergency when parent(s) cannot be reached.

Name _____ Phone_____

Name _____ Phone_____

Page 1 of 2   © 1992 Redleaf Press

A preprinted version of this form is available from Redleaf Press, 800-423-8309.

6. Children with Special Needs

To assure adequate care of _____ , the following is agreed upon:

(name of child)

_____

7. Program Policies: The typical activities for the children are:

Indoor: _____

_____

Outdoor: _____

_____

The infant schedule/activities will be: _____

_____

To insure optimal health and welfare of the child(ren), the parent(s)/legal guardian and provider will use the following methods to communicate concerns on the child(ren)'s progress (keep a notebook of daily happenings, talk on the phone once a week, quarterly conferences, etc.): _____

_____

8. Meals, Naps, Extra Clothing, and Toilet Learning:

The following meals and/or snacks will be provided by the provider: _____

_____

Other food information: _____

_____

Nap and rest policy will be: _____

_____

The following items of extra clothing will be provided by the parent(s)/legal guardian: _____

_____ Cloth diapers _____ Disposable diapers will be provided by (Parent/Legal Guardian or Provider): _____

For toilet learning the parent/legal guardian will supply (training pants, extra changes of clothes, etc.): _____

_____

Potty chair will be provided by (Parent/Legal Guardian or Provider): _____

Feces will be called _____; urine will be called _____;

bowel movements will be called _____; and urinating will be called _____.

9. Discipline Policy: Provider rules for disciplining children will be: _____

_____

10. Other Issues: Other issues of concern to either parent/legal guardian or provider: _____

_____

Page 2 of 2   © 1992 Redleaf Press

No portion of this form may be reproduced without permission of the publisher. Contact Redleaf Press, 450 N. Syndicate, Suite 5, St. Paul, Minnesota 55104, 800-423-8309 for information on purchasing additional copies

III. Acceptance Form

This is to confirm that _____, (name of child)

has been accepted for care by the provider and a place will be reserved until the first day of

care which will begin on _____ (date).

An enrollment fee of $ _____ has been received. This enrollment fee will not be

returned in the event that the child is not placed in care. When the child does begin care, the

enrollment fee will be applied to the _____ week(s) of care.

Date _____

Signature of parent(s)/guardian(s) _____

Signature of provider _____

SAMPLE

IV. Enrollment Form

A. Basic Information

Name of child _____ Birthdate _____

Mother's name _____ Home phone _____

Home address _____

Business address _____

Business phone _____

Father's name _____ Home phone _____

Home address _____

Business address _____

Business phone _____

Child lives with: Mother _____ Father _____ Other _____

Other children living with child:

    Name _____ Age _____ Sex _____

    Name _____ Age _____ Sex _____

    Name _____ Age _____ Sex _____

B. Health History

Check illnesses child has had:

Asthma	☐	Pneumonia	☐
Chicken Pox	☐	Rheumatism	☐
Diabetes	☐	Scarlet Fever	☐
Epilepsy	☐	Strep Throat	☐
Measles	☐	Whooping Cough	☐
Mumps	☐	Other _____	

Allergies (food, drug, bee sting, etc.) list type, symptoms and treatment required _____

_____

Name of child's physician or health clinic _____

Phone of doctor or health clinic _____

SAMPLE

V. Medical Form

This form should be updated annually.

Date _____

1. Basic Information

Name of child _____ Birthdate _____

Mother's name _____ Home phone _____ Business phone _____

Father's name _____ Home phone _____ Business phone _____

Child lives with: ❑ Mother ❑ Father ❑ Other _____

Other children living with child:

Name _____ Age _____ Sex _____

Name _____ Age _____ Sex _____

Name _____ Age _____ Sex _____

2. Health History

Check illnesses child has had or has:

Asthma ❑	Epilepsy ❑	Pneumonia ❑	Strep Throat ❑
Chicken Pox ❑	Measles ❑	Rheumatism ❑	Whooping Cough ❑
Diabetes ❑	Mumps ❑	Scarlet Fever ❑	Other _____

Allergies (food, drug, bee sting, etc.) list type, symptoms, and treatment required _____
_____

Immunization (Date of most recent shot):

Small Pox _____(month/year) Rubella _____(month/year) Polio _____(month/year)

Mumps _____(month/year) Diphtheria _____(month/year) Measles _____(month/year)

Tetanus _____(month/year) Tuberculosis _____(month/year) Other _____

Copy of immunization record attached and signed by doctor: ❑ Yes ❑ No

Date and clinic of last medical exam _____

Does your child have any special needs that require accommodation by the provider? If so, please list _____
_____

Does your child have any functional limitations? (Functional limitations can include, but are not limited to, limitations dealing with hearing, seeing, breathing, speaking, learning, working, performing manual tasks, caring for oneself, social skills, and behavioral actions.) If so, please list_____
_____

Does your child have a condition that, according to current medical information, would pose a direct threat to the health or safety of others in the program? ❑ Yes ❑ No

Page 1 of 2   ©1996 Redleaf Press

A preprinted version of this form is available from Redleaf Press, 800-423-8309.

3. Developmental Background

Name of previous child care program attended _____

Does child have any special problems/fears? _____

Child's favorite activities, foods _____

Child's nap pattern _____

Child's favorite toy or blanket _____

Toilet habits _____

Child's eating habits _____

What makes the child frustrated or upset? _____

Family rules that provider should know about? _____

_____

What methods of discipline do you find work best for your child? _____

_____

4. Medical Emergency Consent

Name of child's physician or health clinic _____

Phone number of doctor or health clinic _____

Medical insurance company _____ Policy # _____

Child's hospital _____ Phone _____

Name of child's dentist _____ Phone _____

When there is a medical emergency, or when a child needs immediate medical treatment, the provider will take all reasonable steps to see that the children in her/his care receive adequate medical care. When appropriate, the provider will call 911 and the parent(s). If the parent(s) cannot be reached, the provider will call the person(s) listed below who are authorized by the parent to give permission for the medical treatment of the child. These person(s) authorized to do so are:

Name _____ Phone _____

Name _____ Phone _____

If the parent(s) and the authorized person(s) cannot be reached, the provider will call the child's doctor, identified above. If the child must be taken to the hospital, the provider will take the child to the child's hospital identified above. If under the circumstances, it is more reasonable to bring the child to another hospital, the provider will do so. In the situation where the parent(s) and the person(s) authorized to give permission for medical treatment are not able to be reached, the parent authorizes the child's doctor to provide the appropriate medical treatment for the child.

Provider's signature _____ Date _____

Mother/Legal Guardian's signature _____ Date _____

Father/Legal Guardian's signature _____ Date _____

If the parent or legal guardian is under age 18, a co-signer must sign this agreement.

Co-signer's signature _____ Date _____

©1996 Redleaf Press

VI. Medication Consent Form

1. Parental Release for Administration of Prescription Medications

Child's name _____

Medication _____

I, _____ (parent/guardian name) give permission for the above
medication to be given to my child only as prescribed by _____.
(name of physician). This medication may be given to the child until _____ (date
or when empty).

Parent/Guardian Signature _____

Date _____

2. Parental Release for Administration of Medication on Doctor's Orders

Child's name _____

Medication _____

Condition for which prescribed_____

Possible side effects _____

Dosage and time of administration_____

Medication to begin _____ (date) until _____(date)

Other remarks _____

Date _____ Doctor Signature _____

Address _____

Phone_____

I request the above medication be given to my child as ordered by the doctor.

Date _____ Parent/Guardian Signature _____

VII. Field Trip Permission Form

A. General Permission Form

_____ (name of provider) may take _____

_____ (name of child(ren) for short walking trips as

part of the family child care program.

Date _____

Parent Signature _____

Address _____

City/Zip _____

B. Specific Permission Form

_____ (name of provider) has my consent to take

_____(name of child(ren) on the

following trip:

Place: _____

Date : _____

Parent Signature _____

Date _____

SAMPLE

VIII. Receipt for Payment Form

BUSINESS RECEIPT FOR CHILD CARE SERVICES   © 1990 Redleaf Press, St. Paul, MN

No. _____   19 _____

Received from _____ $ _____
                                    (parent/guardian name)

_____ Dollars

☐ Cash   For Child Care Services from _____ to _____
☐ Check # _____   M   D   Y   M   D   Y

                                Provider's Signature _____

_____   Parent's Signature _____
Provider's Taxpayer ID# or SS#

A preprinted version of this form is available from Redleaf Press, 800-423-8309.

IX. Parent Evaluation Form

1. What do you like best about how your provider cares for your child?

_____

_____

_____

2. What do you wish your provider would do differently about caring for your child?

_____

_____

_____

3. What else can you suggest that would help your provider do a better job?

_____

_____

_____

4. What actions might you take that would help improve the care of your child when he/she is with your provider?

_____

_____

_____

5. Would you recommend your provider to other parents? Why or why not?

_____

_____

_____

6. Other Comments: _____

_____

_____

Parent's name (optional) _____ Date _____

Child's name _____

X. Other Resources

The Child Care Law Center and Bananas both have a series of publications that are very useful. Write or call them for information about the cost of their publications.

Child Care Law Center
22 Second Street, 5th Floor
San Francisco, California 94105
(415) 495-5498

    Finding and Using Legal Resources for Childcare
    Parent-Provider Contracts
    Child Care Contracts: Information for Parents
    Collecting Fees Owed: Using Small-Claims Court
    Insuring Your Program: Vehicle and Property Insurance
    How to Find and Use a Lawyer

Bananas Child Care Information and Referral
5232 Claremont Avenue
Oakland, California 94618
(510) 658-7101

    Sample Agreement for Parents and Babysitters
    Child Care Complaints
    Parent-Teacher Conferences
    Provider-Parent Contracts
    Making a Difference: A Handbook for Child Care Providers

California Child Care Resources and Referral Network
111 New Montgomery, 7th Floor
San Francisco, California 94105
(415) 823-0234

    Family Child Care Handbook

About the Author

Tom Copeland is the Director of Redleaf National Institute. He has a law degree and has conducted business workshops for family child care providers for over fifteen years. He is also the author of *The Basic Guide to Family Child Care Record Keeping, Teaching Family Child Care Record Keeping and Tax Preparation: A Curriculum for Trainers,* and the *Family Child Care Tax Workbook* (updated annually). His video, *The Business of Family Child Care: How to be Successful in Your Caring Profession* (produced by the Soho Center), offers an introduction to the business responsibilities of providers. All of the above materials are available from Redleaf Press.

Redleaf National Institute

The Institute's mission is to improve the quality of family child care by delivering products and services which strengthen the ability of providers to successfully manage their business.

The Institute offers training, technical assistance, publications, and workshops on record keeping, tax preparation, contracts and policies, marketing, and other legal and business issues. For further information about bringing these business workshops to your area, contact Redleaf National Institute at 612-641-6675.

Also From Redleaf Press
Basic Resources for Your Family Child Care

The Basic Guide to Family Child Care Record Keeping - Easy-to-follow instructions on how to keep all your family child care business records.

The Business of Family Child Care with Tom Copeland - This introductory video covers the seven most important rules for record keeping, as well as taxes, insurance, contracts, and the Food Program. Produced by the Soho Center.

Business Receipts for Child Care Services - Handy receipts designed specifically for family child care. Improve your record keeping and your professional image.

Calendar-Keeper - Streamline your record-keeping needs into a single calendar which also contains activities, recipes, menus, and more. Updated yearly.

Calendar-Keeper Cookbook - A great selection of 100 CACFP-approved recipes from 20 years of Redleaf's popular Calendar-Keeper make this cookbook a hit with providers and the kids in their care.

Family Child Care Contracts and Policies - Learn how to establish and enforce contracts and policies to improve your business.

Family Child Care Tax Workbook - Save time and money and calculate your taxes error free. Includes all new tax information for the year.

The (No Leftovers!) Child Care Cookbook - Contains over 80 kid-tested recipes and 20 complete menus with nutrition information—all CACFP approved. Ideal for larger home-based programs.

Room for Loving, Room for Learning - Put together the space that you need for yourself, your family, and the children in your care with this book full of ingenious ideas for better storage and activity areas.

Sharing in the Caring - A parent/provider agreement packet that helps you establish good business relationships and enhance your professional image. Also available are **Parent/Provider Policies**, actual forms you can use to create a thorough parent agreement, and **Medical Forms**, actual forms for documenting health and medical information on the children in your care—information that is required by most states.

Tips from Tina - Discover how to save yourself cleanup time and make routines more fun with these fresh solutions for those irritating, won't-go-away problems.

To order or for more information call
Redleaf Press
800-423-8309